D0511758

GUIDE TO
LOCOMOTIVES
OF THE WORLD

521 809 59 4

GUIDE TO
LOCOMOTIVES
OF THE WORLD

A GLOBAL ENCYCLOPEDIA
OF THE GREATEST TRAINS

Colin Garratt

HERMES
HOUSE

Acknowledgements

The publishers would like to thank the following for their permission to reproduce their pictures:

A. E. Durrant: pages 109 (m), 112 (m), 114 (tl), 119 (t, m).
Barnaby's Picture Library: pages 52, 53 (tl, b).
Ian D. C. Button: page 83 (b).
H. H. Cartwright: 18 (t).
Alex Grunbach: pages 112 (t), 113, 114 (b), 115, 116, 117.
Ken Harris: page 77 (tl).
Maurice Harvey: page 120 (br).
Fred Hornby: pages 63 (m), 66 (t), 68 (t), 72 (b), 81 (b).

International Railway Journal: pages 84 (bl), 88, 89 (t, m), 120 (br).
Frederick Kerr: page 10 (b).
Alan Pike: pages 54, 55 (t, b), 56 (t, m), 57, 58, 59, 60, 61 (t, b), 62, 63 (t, b), 64 (t, bl), 65 (t), 66 (b), 67, 68 (b), 69, 70, 71, 73, 74, 75, 76, 78, 79, 80 (m, b), 81 (t), 85 (tr).
Graham Pike: pages, 55 (m), 56 (b), 61 (m), 65 (b), 110, 111 (t, m).
William Sharman: pages 24 (t, b), 25.
Brian Solomon: pages 28, 29, 30, 31, 32, 33, 34, 35, 36, 37 (t, b), 38, 39, 40, 41, 42 (b), 43, 44, 45, 46, 47 (b)
Richard J. Solomon: pages 37 (m), 42 (t), 47 (t).

Gordon Stemp: pages 10 (t), 11 (t), 16 (b), 128.
Michael Taplin: pages 22, 104, 105, 106, 107.
J. M. Tolson: pages 108 (m), 109 (t), 122 (t), 123 (br).
Neil Wheelwright: pages, 96, 97, 98, 99, 100, 101, 102, 103, 108 (t, b), 109 (b), 111 (b).
Ron Ziel: pages 82 (b).
Cover photography: **Paolo Curto / The Image Bank** (front), **Michael Melford Inc. / The Image Bank** (back).
All other pictures courtesy of **Milepost 92½**.

Key:
t=top, b=bottom, l=left, r=right, m=middle.

This edition is published by Hermes House, an imprint of Anness Publishing Ltd, Hermes House, 88–89 Blackfriars Road, London SE1 8HA; tel. 020 7401 2077; fax 020 7633 9499

www.hermeshouse.com;
www.annesspublishing.com

Anness Publishing has a new picture agency outlet for images for publishing, promotions or advertising. Please visit www.practicalpictures.com for more information.

Publisher Joanna Lorenz
Editorial Manager Helen Sudell
Project Editor Emma Gray
Designer Michael Morey
Production Controller Mai-Ling Collyer

This book has been written and picture researched by the Milepost Publishing Production Team: Milepost also conserves and markets collections of railway transparencies and negatives.
Milepost 92½, Newton Harcourt, Leicestershire LE8 9FH, UK

ETHICAL TRADING POLICY
At Anness Publishing we believe that business should be conducted in an ethical and ecologically sustainable way, with respect for the environment and a proper regard to the replacement of the natural resources we employ.

As a publisher, we use a lot of wood pulp in high-quality paper for printing, and that wood commonly comes from spruce trees. We are therefore currently growing more than 750,000 trees in three Scottish forest plantations: Berrymoss (130 hectares/320 acres), West Touxhill (125 hectares/305 acres) and Deveron Forest (75 hectares/185 acres). The forests we manage contain more than 3.5 times the number of trees employed each year in making paper for the books we manufacture.

Because of this ongoing ecological investment programme, you, as our customer, can have the pleasure and reassurance of knowing that a tree is being cultivated on your behalf to naturally replace the materials used to make this book.

Our forestry programme is run in accordance with the UK Woodland Assurance Scheme (UKWAS) and will be certified by the internationally recognized Forest Stewardship Council (FSC). The FSC is a non-government organization dedicated to promoting responsible management of the world's forests. Certification ensures forests are managed in an environmentally sustainable and socially responsible way.

For further information about this scheme, go to www.annesspublishing.com/trees

© Anness Publishing Ltd 2000, 2011

All rights reserved. No part of this publication may be reproduced, stored in a retrieval system, or transmitted in any way or by any means, electronic, mechanical, photocopying, recording or otherwise, without the prior written permission of the copyright holder.

A CIP catalogue record for this book is available from the British Library.

Previously published as part of a larger volume, *The World Encyclopedia of Locomotives*

PUBLISHER'S NOTE
For historical reasons, the measurements in this book are not always given with their equivalent metric or imperial measurements. See page 128 for a conversion chart.

Although the information in this book is believed to be accurate and true at the time of going to press, neither the authors nor the publisher can accept any legal responsibility or liability for any errors or omissions that may have been made.

CONTENTS

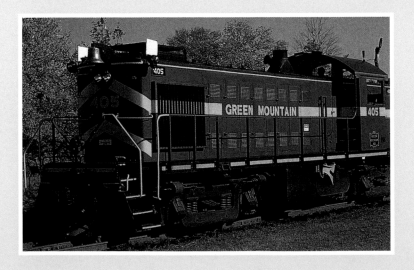

Introduction

The second half of the 20th century saw the decline of the railway as the premier form of transport. Competition from roads and airlines was intense, and vast amounts of railways were closed worldwide. Half-way through the period, the steam locomotive disappeared from much of the world, and in Western countries it became almost extinct. However, railway administrations sought to stave off competition with super hi-tech trains, and today we are seeing a vigorous international movement away from roads and back to rail. Increasing congestion and population are helping railways to make this resurgence.

● **OPPOSITE**
An Australia National (formerly Commonwealth Railways) locomotive resting beside a platform.

● **ABOVE**
An 8,100-hp Class 103 Co-Co, built for the Deutsche Bundesbahn's IC and TEE network, threads through the Rhine Gorge between Bonn and Mainz in the Rhineland-Palatinate state of Germany.

BRITISH MAIN-LINE SHUNTERS AND INDUSTRIALS

The evolution of British main-line steam shunting-locomotives ended in effect in the 1950s. It fell to the Great Western Railway (GWR) to end the tradition formally with its 1500 Class/9400 Class 0-6-0-Ts. Building of the 9400 Class continued until 1956 when it totalled 210 engines. These were the last examples of a pre-nationalization design built by British Railways.

With many 0-6-0Ts inherited from the "Big Four" companies, British Railways had little need for any more shunting-tanks. Downgraded goods-engines became evermore available and

● **LEFT**
American-built diesels are being used on Britain's railways, on the main lines and in industrial service. This example, built for Foster Yeoman, is preparing rakes of aggregates at the company's Merehead quarry.

● **BELOW LEFT**
Several Great Western Railway (GWR) 5700 Class 0-6-0 pannier tanks passed into industrial service, to receive a further lease of life, like this one working at a colliery in South Wales.

gravitated to shunting yards in hundreds. The contemporaneous advent of diesel-shunters in the 1950s saw the standard British Railways diesel-electric 350-hp 0-6-0 produced in profusion from Derby Works, in Derby, Derbyshire. Many remain in service, fulfilling the modest shunting opportunities left on the main-line system.

● **DIESELS REPLACE STEAM SHUNTERS**

It had long been recognized that diesels were superior for shunting. Their ability to switch on and off for work often involving long idle periods showed a clear advantage. Also, the even torque provided sure-footed starts with heavy loads.

Since 1966, there has been a huge fall in the number of shunting-engines. Certainly fewer diesel engines are needed than steam. Far more significant, however, has been the erosion of sidings and marshalling yards as freight has been transferred from rail to road. Instead of the shunter being an everyday sight with thousands operating nationwide, sight of one now is a rare occurrence that often draws comment.

● **RIGHT**
A 16- in Andrew Barclay 0-4-0 saddle-tank draws a rake of freshly lifted coal out of the washery at Pennyvenie Mine, near Dalmellington, Ayrshire, Scotland.

● **PRIVATE USE DECIMATED**

Steam-shunters survived in industrial environments many years after disappearing from main-line service. The last did not entirely disappear until the mid-1980s. Although diesels, including some early British Railway engines, readily infiltrated industrial networks too, the massive decline in Britain's heavy industry and increasing dependence on roads decimated the number of private organizations using their own loco-motives. Those remaining, at collieries and power stations mostly, adopt the merry-go-round principle in which main-line trains serve the industry direct.

Fifty years ago, thousands of steam locomotives were working in hundreds of British collieries. Today there are no steam locomotives and only a handful of active collieries.

● **LEFT**
Cadley Hill Colliery, near Burton on Trent, Staffordshire, central England, was part of the Derbyshire Coalfield and one of the last locations in Britain to use steam locomotives. In this view, with Drakelow Power Station in the background, a standard Hunslet Austerity 0-6-0St (right) shunts beside Progress, a Robert Stephenson & Hawthorn 0-6-0 saddle-tank with inside-cylinders.

CLASS 08 DIESEL SHUNTER

Builder	Derby Locomotive Works, Derby, England
Client	British Railways
Gauge	Standard
Engine	English Electric 6-cylinder 350 brake horsepower (bhp) (261 kW)
Total weight	50 tons
Maximum tractive effort	35,000 lb
Maximum speed	15–20 mph

● **RIGHT**
Penzance, Cornwall, is one location of the British Railway network that retains a shunting-engine – a standard 08 Class Diesel Electric 0-6-0.

BRITISH MAIN-LINE FREIGHT

In the 1950s, many 2-8-0s firmly controlled main freight hauls on the newly formed British Railways. The most numerous were the Great Western Railway's 2800s; the LNER's 01, 02 and 04 classes; Stanier's LMS Class 8F 2-8-0 and their Ministry of Supply version from World War II. In all, these totalled about 2,000 locomotives. The 2-8-0 was supported by a vast array of 0-6-0s and 0-8-0s, which in themselves handled trains little short of 1,000 tons, especially the 0-8-0s of the former North Eastern and London's North Western railways.

The 0-10-0, widely used in Europe, was avoided in Britain. Its light axleload was of little benefit. Its potential power and adhesion for hill-climbing were not generally necessary. The 2-8-0's greater flexibility was preferred.

Similarly, the 2-8-2 and 4-8-0 were not applied. The 2-8-2's wide firebox capacity did not have to be exploited, because of the good quality coal available. The 4-8-0's powerful hill-climbing capacity was not needed on Britain's main lines. Outside the mainstream of

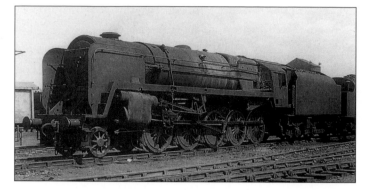

● LEFT
A British Railway's standard Class 9F 2-10-0s, No. 92084, reposes at Cricklewood Depot, north London, in 1960. This class totalled 250 engines.

● LEFT
An ARC's Class 59 Co-Co diesel-electric built in the USA by General Motors. Heavyfreight locomotives for Britain in future are likely to be American-built and of similar proportions to these aggregate-haulers.

● BELOW
Brush of Loughborough's Class 60 Co-Co diesel-electric No. 60061 Alexander Graham Bell heading oil-tanks along the West Coast main line beneath the 25 kV a.c. catinery. The 100 Class 60s, an advanced diesel-electric design, perform heavy haulage with trainloads up to 3,000 tons.

typically heavyfreight designs were some mighty 2-8-0 tanks Churchward produced, to work coal-trains from the valleys of South Wales to the docks.

● **NATIONALIZATION BRINGS STANDARDS**

Fast mixed-freights were pulled by Moguls, 2-6-2s or 4-6-0 types generally regarded as mixed-traffic designs. The LMS Crabs and Gresley K3s were typical Moguls. The V2s were the main design of 2-6-2. The 4-6-0s were epitomized by Stanier's Black 5s of the LMS, Thompson's B1s of the LNER and Collett's Halls of the GWR. The antecedent of the 4-6-0 fast mixed-traffic goes back to the early years of the century with Robinson's Fish engines and Fast Goods types.

Following nationalization of Britain's railways in 1948, 12 standard designs – the Standards – were prepared for the

● **RIGHT**
British Railways Class 56 Co-Co diesel-electric locomotives were introduced in 1977 to handle heavy, slow-speed merry-go-round trains. The first 30 were built in Romania. A further 75 were built at Doncaster, South Yorkshire, and Crewe, Cheshire. The Class 56s have a 16-cylinder Ruston four-stroke diesel engine. The type has become a main heavyfreight hauler on the British Railways network.

CLASS 47 CO-CO DIESEL ELECTRIC

Date	1962
Builder	Brush of Loughborough, Leicestershire, and BR Crewe Works, Crewe, Cheshire, England
Client	British Railways
Gauge	Standard
Engine	Sulzer 1920 kW (2,580 hp)
Total weight	125 tons
Maximum tractive effort	60,000 lb
Maximum speed	95 mph

entire country. Among them was the Class 9F 2-10-0 heavy-mineral engine. So the evolution of the British goods-engine had at the eleventh hour aspired to ten-coupled traction some 50 years after the type had become prevalent in America and 40 years after its inception in Austria and Germany.

The trusted British 0-6-0 drudge had finally turned into a highly sophisticated engine. The 9F presented a perfect climax to British freight-locomotive development. Considering the inside-cylinder 0-6-0's major role over 125 years, it is amazing that its absolute displacement came within such a narrow space of time – the Southern Railway's Q1s appearing only 11 years before the first 9Fs.

The last 9F 2-10-0 was built in 1960. What a contrast these ultimate British freight haulers made with Stephenson's Locomotion No. 1 of 1825.

The diesel engine was invented in 1892 by French-born, German-educated engineer Rudolf Diesel (1858–1913). The first diesel engines were used in ships in 1903. The first diesel locomotive was built at the works of Sulzer in Switzerland in 1913.

● **RIGHT**
The Class 47 Co-Co diesel-electric's versatility is shown in this scene at Harbury Cutting, as one heads a Rail-freight Distribution container-train operating between Birmingham, West Midlands, and Southampton Docks, Hampshire.

BRITISH DIESEL MULTIPLE UNITS (DMUs)

The diesel multiple unit (DMU) descended from steam railcars working on the LMS and LNER in the 1920s and 1930s. These consisted of a single coach with a driving-compartment at either end and a steam-engine encased in a compartment at one end of the coach.

Britain's diesel-cars were introduced by GWR in 1933 for excursion traffic, branch-line and local services. Initially they worked between Paddington in west London and Didcot, about 80 km (50 miles) away in Oxfordshire. In 1934 they were used in an express service, mainly for businessmen on the 155 km (100 miles) between Birmingham in central England and Cardiff in Wales. The trains comprised two railcars with a restaurant-car between. This formation anticipated the first generation of DMUs in having two motor-units with a trailing car between and the later InterCity 125s with a power-car at both ends.

CLASS 158 EXPRESS DMU	
Date	1990
Builder	British Rail Engineering Ltd. (BREL), England
Client	British Rail
Gauge	Standard
Engine	One Cummings 260 kW (350 hp) or 300 kW (400 hp), alternatively Perkins 260 kW (350 hp)
Maximum service speed	90 mph

● **ADVENT OF DIESEL-RAILCAR**

The advent of the diesel-railcar proper was in the 1950s, as part of the British Railways 1955 Modernization Plan. The theory was that diesel-units could serve more stations efficiently, effect rapid starts and use high speeds between stations separated by only a few miles. No sooner had DMUs taken over many steam-stopping services than a vast

● **ABOVE**
A brand-new Turbo Class 165 for working the Chiltern lines between London Marylebone Station and Birmingham reposes outside the Aylesbury depot, Buckinghamshire. These trains were introduced in 1992 as part of the Chiltern lines' total route modernization.

● **LEFT**
A Class 158 two-car BREL express unit. This design has bridged the gap between local/cross-country work and express services and is used on many long-distance runs across Britain.

number of stations were closed nationwide under Beeching.

Early, steel-bodied DMUs ran as two-, three- or four-coach units. Two-car ones generally comprised two motor-units. Three-car ones had a trailing unit in between. Four-car ones had a motor-unit at both ends. The diesel engine sat beneath the motorized cars, providing direct drive.

Many designs appeared in the 1950s and 1960s, particularly from the works at Derby and Swindon, Wiltshire, and from private builders such as Metro Cammell, Birmingham Railway Carriage and Wagon Co. and Cravens. These early units were known later as Heritage DMUs. Their numbers ever dwindle but several classes remain in service.

● SECOND GENERATION

The second-generation DMU was introduced in the mid-1980s as the Sprinter series. These have sliding doors, hydraulic transmissions and offer great advance in riding qualities over the earlier trains. The main classes are the 150s and the 156s. Both are usually seen in two-car formations and have a Cummins 285 hp engine beneath each car.

In contrast came the Pacers embraced by Classes 141, 142 and 143/144. These are lighter, four-wheeled vehicles with each car motorized. The absence of bogies made these units rougher to ride in and probably accounts

for why they have not been popular.

The pièce de résistance of British DMUs is the Class 158 express unit. This first appeared from British Rail Engineering Ltd (BREL) in 1990. The 158s consist of two car units with an advanced bogie design and a 350 hp engine per car. They perform well on medium- and long-distance runs, are extremely comfortable and have a 90 mph top speed.

This second generation of DMUs has gone into widespread service nationwide and all but replaced traditional locomotive-hauled trains.

● **ABOVE LEFT**
First-generation heritage DMUs, in Network South East livery repose at London Marylebone depot while working the Chiltern line. These units have been replaced on Thames and Chiltern lines by Class 165 Turbo-DMUs operating from the new depot at Aylesbury, Buckinghamshire.

● **ABOVE RIGHT**
A Class 141 Leyland Pacer in West Yorkshire (Public Transport Executive [PTE]) livery. These units were built from Leyland National Bus parts on four-wheeled underframes at the Derby works, Derby, in 1984.

● **BELOW**
A green-liveried Heritage DMU "bubble car" heads an afternoon local service between Bletchley, Buckinghamshire, and Bedford, in the Midlands. Classified 121, these units date from 1960.

BRITISH ELECTRICAL MULTIPLE UNITS (EMUs)

The electrical multiple unit (EMU) predated the diesel multiple unit (DMU) by many years for the City & South London Railway, which used EMUs when it opened in 1890. Power-collection was from a third rail carrying 450 volts. Apart from London's Underground, it was the Southern Railway – following the 1923 Grouping – which truly exploited the EMU's potential with an expanding network of electrification based on a third-rail system at 600 volts d.c.

In 1923, Britain's railway companies had been reorganized into four groups – the "Big Four": London, Midland & Scottish (LMS); London & North Eastern (LNER); the Great Western (GWR) and the Southern Railway (SR).

EMUs' high power:weight ratio provides the rapid acceleration needed on busy suburban services. Most EMUs consist of four-car sets including a motor-coach. As traffic demands, these trains can be run as either four-, eight- or 12-coach combinations.

● NEW GENERATION

As main-line electrification spread across Britain from the late-1950s, a new

● LEFT
Among British vintage overhead EMUs are Class 302s. One is pictured leaving Fenchurch Street Station, London, for Essex on the London-Tilbury, Southend-on-Sea section. These date back to the 1950s.

● ABOVE
A former Network South East Class 415/6. These are among the oldest units left on Britain's railways. They are slam-door stock with 750 volt d.c. third rail and date back to 1959.

● BELOW
Class 323s were introduced in 1992 for the West Midlands Public Transport Executive (PTE) and Greater Manchester PTE areas. They have aluminium bodies, thyristor control and sliding doors.

generation of EMUs emerged with overhead pantographs collecting from 25 kV a.c. More recently dual-voltage units have appeared, capable of running on 25 kV a.c. overhead and 750 volt d.c. third rail. In this category, Thameslink Class 319 and 319/1s operate between Bedford, in the Midlands, and Brighton, the Sussex seaside resort, through the heart of London.

In the 1950s, DMU and EMU features were combined to produce several classes of trains with a diesel-engine in the motor-coach to generate electricity to drive the traction motors. These diesel electrical multiple units (DEMUs) run on sections of non-electrified railway.

● SUPERFAST EXPRESSES

In common with the DMU, the EMU soon developed into express units, the Brighton Belle being an early example. More recently, the Wessex Electrics have been introduced and operate superfast services between London Waterloo and Southampton in Hampshire and Bournemouth and Weymouth in Dorset. Later, the Networker Express Class 365, with aluminium bodies, advanced bogie design and regenerative braking, were introduced. These are 100 mph express units of comfort and sophistication.

● **RIGHT**
An express Class 325 parcels unit for postal services, with roller-shutter doors, heads south through the Lune Gorge with a West Coast postal train. These units operate on 25 kV a.c. overhead, 750 volt d.c. third rail.

● **BELOW**
Class 465 Networker EMUs replaced ageing units on Kent Link services. The new units have aluminium bodies, sliding doors and regenerative braking. They entered service in the early-1990s when building of new trains was at an all-time low. In 1996, the Class C1365 Networker Express was launched by Connex South Eastern. These 100-mph trains have dual-voltage capability, 2+2 seating layout (2+3 on Kent Link), a toilet for the disabled and carpeting throughout.

● **BELOW**
The Wessex Electrics Class 442 is a most prestigious EMU. These 100 mph units were built for the Waterloo-Bournemouth-Weymouth services and also worked to Portsmouth Harbour, Hampshire. Unusually for British EMUs, many are named. These comfortable riding units were introduced in 1988 as a partial refurbishment of older stock, a precedent likely to be followed in preference to building new trains.

● **BELOW RIGHT**
A ThamesLink dual-voltage Class 319 climbs the steep gradient into Blackfriars Station, London, with a Bedford-to-Brighton service. These 100 mph units work on 25 kV a.c. on the Midland main line and on 750 volt d.c. on the London-Brighton section.

Class 325 express postal units were introduced in 1995. Apart from their dual voltage, these 100 mph trains are compatible with diesel-locomotive haulage over non-electrified sections, giving access to the entire railway system.

Many units on the 750 volt d.c. lines of southern England are ageing. In 1996,

Adtranz proposed the Networker Classic, a "half-life, quarter-cost solution" to unlock the potential of existing vehicles more than 25 years old by refurbishing the underframe, traction system and running-gear with the latest body design, including automatic sliding doors and crashworthy front ends.

CLASS 319 EMU

Date	1987
Builder	British Rail Engineering (BREL), York, England
Client	British Rail
Gauge	Standard
Engine	Four GEC of 247.1 kw
Maximum tractive effort	35,000 lb
Maximum service speed	100 mph

BRITISH STEAM STANDARDS

On nationalization of the "Big Four" railway companies – LMS, LNER, GWR and SR – in 1948, the new administration inherited hundred of different locomotive types. Many of these had come down from the multiplicity of private companies that existed before the 1923 Grouping. This was untenable for a new, centralized administration and so it was proposed to build 12 standard types – the Standards – to fulfil most functions across the network.

● 1955 MODERNIZATION PLAN

Within four years of the Standards' introduction, the Modernization Plan for 1955 decreed the end of steam in favour of diesel and electric traction. This resulted in the Standards adding even more design variety. The new engines were designed on experience gained by the locomotive exchanges of 1948, in which the Big Four's leading types were tested across one another's territories to ascertain best-performance characteristics. Mechanically and

● LEFT
British Railways Standard 80000 Class 2-6-4Ts were based on earlier LMS engines by Stanier and Fairburn. Powerful, with a turn of speed, they were to be found on many parts of Britain's railway network. The class totalled 155 examples.

BR BRITANNIA PACIFIC 4-6-2

Date	1951
Builder	Crewe Locomotive Works, Crewe, Cheshire, England
Client	British Railways
Gauge	Standard
Driving wheels	6 ft 2 in
Capacity	Cylinders 20 x 28 in
Total weight in full working order	150 tons

aesthetically, the new designs showed a distinct departure from traditional British practices, towards those of America.

The 12 types comprised three Pacifics (the Britannia for fast express work, the Clans for fast mixed-traffic work and the solitary Duke of Gloucester intended as forerunner of a new generation of heavy express-passenger-locomotives), two classes of 4-6-0s, three of Moguls, one powerful 2-6-4 tank, two 2-6-2 tanks and the Class 9F mineral-hauling 2-10-0s.

Except for Duke of Gloucester and the 9Fs, the new Standards were all mixed-traffic designs, because by this time the concept of different locomotives for freight and passenger work had all but

● **RIGHT**
British Railways Standard Pacific No. 71000 Duke of Gloucester reposes outside the paintshop at Crewe Works, Cheshire.

● **BELOW**
British Railways Standard Class 4 4-6-0s were for light passenger and general duties. The class numbered 80 engines. Their clean, modern lines, with distinct American characteristics, are shown in this picture.

● **OPPOSITE BOTTOM**
British Railways Standard Britannia Class Pacific No. 70042 Lord Roberts at Willesden, west London, in 1962.

appeared at the Festival of Britain in 1951, attracting much interest and admiration. This was justified by the Britannias' performance over their relatively short lives. They proved extremely fast engines and put in scintillating performances, not least on the former Great Eastern main line between London Liverpool Street and Norwich, Norfolk.

Perhaps the biggest disappointment, at least initially, was the Duke of Gloucester, sluggish in service and heavy on coal. This engine passed into preservation, having been rescued from Woodhams Scrapyard in Barry, Glamorganshire, South Wales, and renovated to full working order.

Computer calibrations of the Duke's valve settings proved, in the light of contemporary experience, that these were incorrectly set during the engine's main-line years, and the modifications made under preservation have enabled the Duke to climb the notorious Shap Bank with a 450-ton train at a speed hitherto unknown and to top the summit at 51 mph. This gives insight into the potential of steam and of this express-passenger design destined to remain as a solitary engine.

● **BELOW**
British Railways Standard Class 3 Mogul, No. 76005, one of a class of 115 engines for light intermediate work, at Bournemouth Shed, Dorset, in the mid-1960s.

disappeared. In principle, the 9Fs were the exceptions to this rule. In practice, their balanced proportions enabled them to undertake fast running with passenger-trains. Stories abounded of them reaching 90 mph – until their use on such work was forbidden.

● BRITANNIA AT THE FESTIVAL OF BRITAIN

In terms of easy accessibility to moving-parts and labour-saving devices, the Standards were an improvement on most previous designs. In terms of overall performance, they were little different from their Big Four counterparts on which they were largely based.

The first engine, No. 70000 Britannia,

BRITISH DIESEL

The decision to dieselize came rather late in Britain. Not until 1955, when the government announced the Modernization Plan, was the end of the steam age seriously suggested. Even then, prolific railway experts like Cecil J. Allen confidently said steam would last until the end of the century.

The modernization programme was rapidly implemented. This resulted in many classes of diesel appearing, not all of which proved satisfactory. From the outset, diesel-electric was the preferred mode, following extensive trials of the LMS's 1947-built 10000/10001. The brief visit to the concept of diesel-mechanical, as epitomized by H.G. Ivatt's 4-8-4 No. 10100 introduced in 1951, and visits to gas turbines were not continued.

Diesel-hydraulic gained acceptance, especially on former Great Western lines, but the classes concerned, revered as they were, had a short life.

● EARLY EXPERIMENT

Another early experiment was the blue English Electric Deltic, prototype for the

● **LEFT**
H.G. Ivatt's twin diesel-electrics Nos. 10000/10001 appeared in the late 1940s and paved the way for main-line dieselization. This proved to be a milestone in the evolution of British locomotives. A unit is pictured receiving attention in Derby works, Derbyshire.

● **LEFT**
The Class 47 Co-Co diesel "Maid of all Work" has been a familiar sight on Britain's railways since the early 1960s, with hundreds still operating. Here, one leaves Birmingham in the Midlands at the head of a cross-country express.

● **BELOW**
One of the oldest diesel types left on British Railways is the Class 31 Brush Type 2s, introduced by Brush Traction at Loughborough, Leicestershire, in 1957. Over the years, they have been used on a wide variety of duties but are now almost entirely relegated to engineers' trains.

Deltics on the East Coast main line. These were highly admired, extremely successful and proved worthy successors to Gresley's A4 Pacifics.

Fine general-purpose mixed-traffic haulers are the Brush Sulzer Class 47s, which proved worthy successors to the 842 Stanier Black 5s. The 47s proved themselves equally at home with 90 mph passenger-trains or 1,000 ton freight-hauls. About 500 went into service; many remain active.

Other notables include Class 40 English Electrics, which moved most trains on the West Coast main line before electrification, and the Sulzer 12-cylinder Peaks introduced in 1959, which also proved themselves on passenger and freight. The 40s and Peaks are history but the Class 37, a 1950s design built from 1960 onwards, remains an important class engaged on such diverse services as EPS sleeping-car trains, locals, all types of mixed-freight operations and engineers' service trains.

BR CLASS 37 CO-CO DIESEL ELECTRIC

Date	1960
Builder	English Electric Company, Vulcan Factory, Newton-le-Willows, or Robert Stephenson & Hawthorn, Darlington, Durham, England
Client	British Railways
Gauge	Standard
Engine	English Electric 1,300 kW (1,750 hp)
Total weight	108 tons
Maximum tractive effort	55,500 lb
Maximum service speed	80 mph

● **ABOVE RIGHT**
English Electric Type 3 Class 37 Co-Co diesel electrics were built in 1960-65 by the English Electric Co. at its Vulcan Foundry, Lancashire, and by Robert Stephenson & Hawthorn in Darlington, Durham. They truly are maids of all work, fulfilling many functions. One of their most prestigious services is the sleeping-car run through the Scottish Highlands to the tourist attractions of Fort William and Inverness.

● **MIXED-TRAFFIC CONCEPT**

The concept of mixed-traffic locomotives established by the British Railways Standard steam designs has continued through the diesel age, but since 1976 the classes 56, 58 and 60 have been put into operation mainly for mineral- and aggregate-haulage.

The next batches of new diesels for Britain's railways are tipped to come from North America when EWS begin their mighty restocking of British freight-motive power. The new engines may follow the lead begun with Foster Yeoman and ARC's Class 59 General Motors Co-Cos.

● **LEFT**
A Class 50 Co-Co English Electric Type 4 diesel. Built in 1967–68 by the Vulcan Foundry at Newton-le-Willows, Lancashire, these engines originally worked the northern reaches of the West Coast main line between Crewe, in Cheshire, and Carlisle, in Cumbria, but ended up on the South Western main line between London Waterloo and Exeter, Devon.

● **LEFT**
The InterCity 125, one of the most successful trains in British railway history, revolutionized long-distance passenger services. Introduced in 1976, the 125s have a maximum speed of 125 mph, hence their name. A set on the Midland line is seen passing Milepost 92$\frac{1}{2}$, south of Leicester, with a Sheffield-to-London train.

BRITISH MAIN-LINE ELECTRIC

● **BELOW**

● **BELOW**
A Class 73 Bo-Bo electro-diesel in InterCity livery working the Gatwick Express between London Victoria and Gatwick Airport – London, in West Sussex. Built at Eastleigh, near Southampton, Hampshire, in 1962, these engines operate from 660 to 850 volt d.c. third rail and are equipped with an English Electric diesel engine for running over non-electrified sections.

Although it is fashionable for electrification to be thought of as the ultimate railway modernization, it is a form of motive power extant in Britain since the 1880s. In the 19th century, two locomotive engineers, George Stephenson and F.W. Ebb, predicted that one day Britain's railways would run on electricity.

In 1905, the first freight-hauling electric locomotive appeared, on the North Eastern Railway (NER). After that, many adventurous schemes were proposed, including electrification of the NER's main line between York and Newcastle upon Tyne following World War I. However, the Depression in the 1930s, followed by World War II, prevented many projects being started. In 1948, only 17 main-line electric locomotives were inherited by British Railways.

● **GREAT CENTRAL MAIN LINE ELECTRIFIED**

In the early 1950s, a project was continued that had been held over in the war years. This was the electrification to 1,500 volt d.c. overhead of the steeply graded Great Central main line between the English industrial centres of Sheffield in West Yorkshire and Manchester in Lancashire. This highly acclaimed, much-

publicized project operated Bo-Bo locomotives for freight and Co-Co for passengers.

Simultaneously, in the mid-1950s there was a development with Southern Region's electro-diesels. The traction motors were fed from either a third rail or by current generated from an on-board diesel engine, enabling them to run across non-electrified sections. Many of these Class 73s remain active today and can be seen on the Gatwick Express service from London Victoria to Gatwick Airport – London, in West Sussex.

● **WEST AND EAST COAST MAIN LINES ELECTRIFIED**

The West Coast main line, from London Euston Station, is Britain's busiest. It was an early candidate for electrification to 25 kV a.c. under the 1955 modernization scheme. The locomotives were designated mixed-traffic and designed to haul 475-ton trains at 90 mph on level track, with maximum speed of 100 mph, and 950-ton freight-trains at 42 mph, with a 55-mph maximum. The West Coast fleet's mainstay are Class 86s, dating back to 1965. The 86s and later

● **RIGHT**
The 30-year-old Class 86 electric, built by English Electric at the Vulcan Foundry, remain the mainstay of services on the West Coast main line. Here, one approaches Crewe from the south, beneath the 25 kV a.c. overhead catinery.

● **RIGHT**
Driving-van trailers (DVTs) used on Britain's
East Coast and West Coast main lines simulate
the design of Class 91 electrics. On both
routes, southbound trains are headed by
DVTs, as in this London-bound service waiting
to leave Crewe, Cheshire.

● **OPPOSITE MIDDLE**
In the mid-1990s, Class 92 Bo-Bo electrics
were introduced for through-services between
Britain and Europe. The picture shows No.
92.019 at Crewe Station, Cheshire.

BR CLASS 91 BO-BO ELECTRIC

Date	1988
Builder	British Rail Engineering Ltd. (BREL),Crewe Works, Cheshire, England
Client	British Railways
Gauge	Standard
Traction motors	General English Electric (GEC) G426AZ
Total weight	84 tons
Continuous Rating	4540 kW (6090 hp)
Maximum speed	140 mph

87s are augmented by powerful Class 90s
introduced in 1987.

Completion of the East Coast main-
line electrification brought the Crewe-
built Class 91s with an outstanding
140-mph top speed. These are Britain's
most powerful locomotives capable of
running across the East Coast racing-
ground to reach Edinburgh, Scotland, in
under four hours from King's Cross
Station, London.

Almost all West Coast and East Coast
main-line electric services have the
locomotive at one end and a driving-van
trailer (DVT) at the other. These are
basically a luggage-and-parcel van with
a driving console that enables the train to
be driven in either direction without
turning around.

Soon after completion of the 91 class
came the dual-voltage Class 92s for
operating freight- and passenger-trains
through the Channel Tunnel between
Britain and France. Apart from being
another technical triumph, the 92s open
up the possibility of running through
freight-trains from many parts of Britain
directly into Europe.

● **RIGHT**
A GEC-designed
Class 91 Bo-Bo
electric at King's
Cross Station,
London. These
powerful
locomotives
revolutionized
services on the East
Coast main line.

BRITISH LIGHT RAIL

Britain's first electric tramway ran in Blackpool, Lancashire. It was the only British urban tramway to survive the abandonment completed nationwide in Britain by 1962. This traditional system continues to modernize its infrastructure and trams. It is one of only three systems in the world to use double-deck cars.

● TRAMWAYS AND MASS-TRANSIT SYSTEMS

In addition to tramways, mass-transit systems were built in London and Glasgow, Scotland. London Underground is one of the world's largest metro systems, with two sizes of rolling stock used, on subsurface and tube lines respectively. The Glasgow underground is a city-circle line built for cable traction but electrified in the 1930s. New rolling stock was delivered as part of complete modernization in 1978–80.

● TYNE & WEAR METRO

After a decade when it seemed that most of Britain's towns and cities would have

● **BELOW**
Supporting the regeneration of Birkenhead's docklands in Merseyside is a Heritage tramway featuring traditional double-deck trams, but built in Hong Kong to the British style.

to make do with buses and increasing traffic congestion, the late 1970s saw planning start for flexible and cost-effective light-rail systems (LRS). In Tyneside, north-east England, the closure of run-down local rail services offered the Passenger Transport Executive (PTE) the opportunity to create a rail-based

integrated system in 1980–84 by the introduction of light rail and new subways under the city centre. The successful Tyne & Wear Metro has been extended to Newcastle Airport, and also from Sunderland to South Hylton, using the disused Sunderland to Durham line.

● LONDON'S DLR

A different version of light rail was installed in London's Docklands in 1984–7. The Docklands Light Railway (DLR) was built as a fully segregated system (mostly on new or existing viaducts) with third-rail current collection and automatic train operation. Designed to carry 2,000 passengers an hour in single cars, the system soon had to be rebuilt to carry up to 12,000 passengers an hour with multiple-unit trains. The line now extends from Tower Gateway to the Royal Docks Victoria, Albert and King George V on Plaistow Marshes; from Canning Town to Beckton and King George V; to Lewisham; and to

● **LEFT**
Blackpool's Promenade tramway is just the place for a summer ride on an open-top tram. No. 706 is the only double-decker rebuilt to its original, 1935, condition.

SOUTH YORKSHIRE LOW-FLOOR TRAM

Date	1993–4
Builder	Siemens-Duewag, Germany
Gauge	1,435 mm
Power supply	750 v or kV
Bogie arrangement	B-B-B-B with 4x277 kW motors
Overall length	34.75 m
Width	2.65 m
Body height	3.64 m. Floor height 480 mm (880 mm over bogies)
Unladen weight	46.5 tons
Passengers	Seated 88; standing 155
Maximum speed	80 kph

● **LEFT**
South Yorkshire Supertram's steep gradients are easily handled by its German-built low-floor trams. This scene shows the Woodburn Road crossing in the background.

● **BELOW LEFT**
London's Docklands Light Railway (DLR) expanded when the towering office complex at Canary Wharf was built. The complex is served by this station incorporated in the tower.

● **BELOW RIGHT**
The Tyne & Wear Metro in north-east England has taken over local rail services, around Newcastle upon Tyne, including this former freight line to Callerton. It is seen here at Fawdon. The cars were built by Metro Cammell and based on a German design.

Stratford in East London. The system is operated by Serco Docklands Ltd, a company formed jointly by Serco and the former management company, the London Docklands Development Corporation (LDDC).

● **MANCHESTER METROLINK**
In Manchester, light rail was created in 1990–93 by the PTE taking over the rail lines to Bury, Lancashire, and Altrincham, Cheshire, and linking them with new street-track through the city centre.
The system was built and operated by the Metrolink consortium, using articulated trams made by Firema, Italy.

● **SOUTH YORKSHIRE, WEST MIDLANDS AND CROYDON**
In South Yorkshire, a tramway was created in 1992–5 to link Sheffield city centre with outer suburbs and the Meadowhall retail centre. The system's steep gradients required articulated trams with all axles motored. German-built, they are the first trams in Britain to feature low-floor boarding and alighting at all doors. After a slow start, caused by population shifts, poor traffic priorities and bus competition, Sheffield Supertram saw a 40 per cent rise in use in the second half of 1996.

BRITISH TRAIN PRESERVATION

Britain's railway preservation movement was created on 11 October 1950 when a meeting in Birmingham presided over by L.T.C. Rolt declared its intention to save the Talyllyn Railway in Brecknockshire, Central Wales (now Powys). There were no precedents for such action and tremendous opposition came from many sources declaring "enthusiasts could never run a railway". This pioneering endeavour's success is well known among railway enthusiasts.

GREAT WESTERN KING CLASS 4-6-0	
Date	1927
Builder	Swindon Locomotive Works, Wiltshire, England
Client	Great Western Railway (GWR)
Gauge	Standard
Driving wheels	6 ft 6 in
Capacity	4 cylinders (16 x 28 in)
Total weight in full working order	136 tons

● BELOW
Before Deltics were introduced, A4s held sway on the East Coast main line. Here, preserved, is No. 4498 Sir Nigel Gresley, named after the famous locomotive designer. Sir Nigel Gresley (1876–1941) was chief mechanical engineer of England's Great Northern Railway (GNR) and its successor LNER. He designed Mallard.

● RIGHT
Former British Rail Class 55 Co-Co Deltics were a production version of the Deltic prototype locomotive of the mid-1950s. They worked the heaviest long-distance trains on the East Coast main line for many years. Their popularity rendered them a perfect subject for preservation.

● BELOW
Great Western Railway's King Class 4-6-0 express-passenger-engine. Apart from one engine in 1908, GWR did not use Pacifics. Nothing larger than the 4-6-0 was needed, because of the high-quality Welsh coal they burned and the relative flatness of their routes. Several have been preserved. No. 6000 King George V, the original engine of 1927, pictured during "GWR 150" celebrations in 1985.

● **RIGHT**
A former Southern Railway (SR) King Arthur Class 4-6-0, No. 777 Sir Lamiel, *en route* for Leeds and York with the Red Rose Special train.

● **BELOW**
This former LMS Jubilee class 4-6-0, No. 5690 Leander, is one of many examples of preserved locomotives running on British Rail's main lines.

● **BOTTOM**
Unrebuilt "Bulleid Pacific" No. 34092 City of Wells is prepared for the Golden Arrow trip to Leeds, Yorkshire.

PRESERVATION AND THE LEISURE INDUSTRY

So began a movement that over the next 50 years created a vast new leisure industry and saved part of the railway heritage in living form for future generations to enjoy.

Once the 1955 railway modernization programme took effect, class after class of Britain's locomotive heritage was scrapped. A limited selection of loco-motives was earmarked for static display in museums, but this would have done little justice to the heritage, and the joy and wonder of seeing steam trains in action would have been but a dream.

Nationwide, thousands of enthusiasts united to save locomotives, rolling stock and sections of railway. Following the Beeching programme, innumerable closed branch lines were available. Over the years, dozens became the subject of preservation schemes. The movement gained momentum at the ending of steam operation on British Railways on 11 August 1968, after which it was announced that no preserved locomotive would be allowed to run on the national system.

STEAM EXCURSIONS

Today, Britain has more than 100 centres where steam-trains can be enjoyed. They attract millions of visitors every year. More than 2,000 locomotives have been preserved.

Railway preservation is a creative, on-going process. As the first generation of diesels began to slip into history, examples were saved and put to work on preserved lines – often beside the very steam-locomotives they had replaced.

The decision to ban steam was rescind-ed in 1971. Many historic locomotives returned to the main line, including examples borrowed from the National Railway Museum in York. In 1985, a total of 235 steam-excursions operated on British Rail, attracting many people to linesides and promoting awareness of the railway among the general public.

A visit to any preserved line is an unforgettable experience, for enthusiast or lay person alike. These centres achieve authenticity and fascinate all ages.

The union of free enterprise and enthusiasm provided a catalyst for achieving the impossible. Britain's railway preservation movement has been little less dynamic in spirit than Victorian industrialists of a century earlier. The number preserved contrasts with the "handful of stuffed and mounted exhibits" proposed by the Government when the dismantling of the railways began.

EUROSTAR

The idea that steam is exciting while modern traction is dull and lifeless is disproved for ever by Eurostar. This train combines the romance of the 1930s' streamlined era and the cutting edge of technology. London's St Pancras International Station is as magnificent as its Victorian counterpart and the Channel Tunnel, within the 37.5 km (24 mile) terminal-to-terminal fixed link between Folkestone and Calais, is one of the world's greatest civil-engineering feats.

● WORLD'S MOST COMPLEX TRAIN

The connecting of Britain's 16,000 km (10,000 miles) of railway with Europe's 185,000 km (116,000 miles) in 1993 has

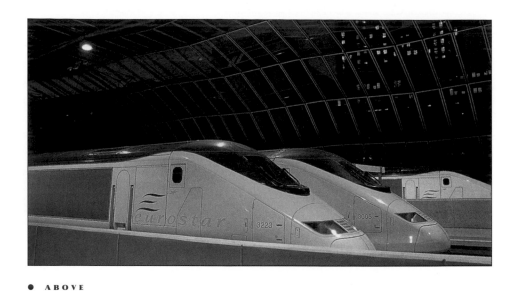

● ABOVE
Three Eurostar units in repose at the former Eurostar terminal at Waterloo International, London, England.

● BELOW
A Eurostar train speeds through the countryside of northern France on the high-speed line.

provided a much-needed and massive boost for railways. Eurostar competes with airlines between the cities of London, Paris and Brussels.

Eurostar is the world's most complex train. It operates on four different signalling systems and three different power-supply systems – 750 volt d.c. 25 kV a.c. in Britain; 25 kV a.c. in the

● **LEFT**
A Eurostar train
from London
approaches the
Channel Tunnel. The
Dolland's Moor
freight complex is in
the background and
a new Class 92
locomotive in the
left foreground.

● **BELOW**
Eurostar trains
waiting to leave
Waterloo
International for
France and Belgium.

● **BOTTOM**
Eurostar design
details.

EUROSTAR

Date	1992
Builder	GEC Alsthom at various works
Clients	British Rail (BR); Société Nationale des Chemins de Fer Français (SNCF); Société Nationale des Chemins de Fer Belges (SNCB)
Gauge	Standard
Traction motors	Six XABB 6PH
Maximum service speed	187.5 mph

tunnel, France and on high-speed lines in
Belgium and 3,000 kV d.c. on Belgium's
conventional network.

● HIGH-SPEED LINK

Eurostar trains comprise 18 coaches.
The trains, at 394 metres (1,293 ft), are
almost a quarter of a mile long. Eurostar
runs at 186 mph on Europe's high-speed
lines but is restricted to below 100 mph
in Britain.

Eurostar's coaches are joined by
bogies. No bogies are set beneath the
passenger seating. This and pneumatic
suspension ensures a smooth, quiet ride.
The train is comfortable and has footrests,
reading-lights and air-conditioning. First-
class has areas for business meetings.

There are two bar-buffets and a trolley
service. Eurostar trains are serviced in
London at the dedicated depot at Temple
Mills, which is located near Stratford
International station.

● OVERNIGHT TRAVEL REVOLUTION

The Eurostar service will be augmented
by two developments. Firstly, day trains
will run between Edinburgh, Manchester,
Birmingham and Paris. Second, night
trains will operate with sleeping-cars.
These services will revolutionize long-
distance overnight travel in Europe.
Passengers will be able to go to bed in
departure cities and awake at their
destination next morning.

AMERICAN SWITCHERS

Switchers, that is engines to transfer rolling stock from one railway track to another, are relatively small, lightweight locomotives in the 300 hp to 1,500 hp range, designed to work at slow speeds, often on poor or winding track.

● FIRST SUCCESSFUL DIESEL-ELECTRIC

The first successful application of diesel-electric locomotives was as switchers. Central Railroad of New Jersey, USA, operated the first commercially successful diesel-electric in 1925. By the 1940s, builders were constructing low-horsepower diesel-electric switchers for yard switching, industrial switching and passenger-terminal work. General Electric (GE), Baldwin, the Electro-Motive Division (EMD) of General Motors, American Locomotive Company (Alco), Fairbanks-Morse, Whitcomb, Porter and Davenport all built switchers in the 1940s and 1950s.

● CHANGING DEMAND

As traffic patterns changed between the 1950s and 1970s, fewer switchers were needed. American railroads discontinued

● **BELOW**
Southern Pacific Lines embraced the switcher longer than other Western railroads and ordered larger numbers of EMD's SW1500s. The 1,500 hp SW1500 was eventually replaced in EMD's catalogue by the MP15, also rated at 1,500 hp.

● **ABOVE**
Baldwin switcher S-12 No. 16 is lettered for the Feather River & Western railroad. Baldwin built more than 550 S-12 diesel-electric switchers of 1,200 hp between 1951-56.

● **LEFT**
A former Alco S-1 switcher of the United States Army poses as Western Pacific Railroad's No. 512. More than 500 S-1s were built for use in the USA and Mexico between 1940-50. The locomotive features a six-cylinder 539 prime mover that delivered 660 hp.

● **RIGHT**
Western Pacific Railroad's NW2u shows off a coat of orange paint at Portola, California. Electro-Motive built 1,119 NW2 switchers of 1,000 hp. Many were later rebuilt, using the "u" designation.

many passenger-trains and thus had a greatly reduced need for switchers at terminals. Carload-freight declined as railroads switched to intermodal operations, that is using different modes of conveyance in conjunction. By the mid-1970s, railroads had stopped ordering large numbers of new switchers. Instead, they either rebuilt existing switchers or downgraded older road-switchers.

● **SWITCHER MODELS**
Electro-Motive began building switchers in the 1930s. An early model that gained popularity was the 1,000 hp NW2 made in 1930–49. The SW1, a 600-hp switcher, was made between 1939-53. Other SW-type switchers, ranging from the 700-hp SW7 to the 1,500-hp SW1500, were made through the 1970s. In the mid-1970s, EMD introduced its 1,500 MP line of switchers.

Alco made many S Series low-

SW8 DIESEL-ELECTRIC	
Date	1950–54
Builder	General Motors (Electro-Motive Division)
Engine	8-cylinder 567B
Capacity	567cc per cylinder
Power	800 hp

horsepower switchers between 1940–60. General Electric built switchers for many years before entering the heavy road locomotive market in 1960. Its most popular switchers were its 44-ton and 70-ton models.

In the 1990s, builder Morrison-Knudsen entered the new-switcher market with conventionally powered diesel-electrics and natural gas-powered locomotives. By 1996, it had not sold more than a handful of locomotives.

● **RIGHT**
An SW8 of the Wellsboro & Corning Railroad leads a train south of Gang Mills, New York. The EMD's 800-hp SW8 was built between 1950–54. Many short lines prefer switchers to larger road-switcher locomotives.

AMERICAN TRAINS IN THE 1950S

American freight railroads have relied on diesel-electric locomotives to move the bulk of their tonnage since America saw the end of steam in the 1950s. Builders have implemented many improvements in locomotive design in the last 40 years. Locomotive-builders — now just General Motor's Electro-Motive Division (EMD) and General Electric (GE) — have been working on single-engine, single-unit locomotives with ever-greater pulling power.

● HORSEPOWER RACE

In the 1950s, EMD's GP9 road-switcher and F9 carbody locomotives were state-of-the-art designs, each developing 1,750 hp with a 567-series 16-cylinder prime mover and traditional d.c. traction motors.

In the early 1960s, EMD increased the 567 prime mover's horsepower by adding a turbocharger, featured on its GP20 and SD24 models. Meanwhile, General Electric entered the new heavy-haul diesel-electric locomotive market

● **LEFT**
General Electric (GE) surpassed its main competitor, EMD, in new-locomotive sales with the introduction of the DASH-8 line. One of Santa Fe Railroad's 4,000 hp DASH 8-40Bs rests in Corwith yard, Chicago, Illinois.

● **ABOVE**
Brand-new EMD SD70MAC locomotives in Chicago. Burlington Northern Railroad prefers these powerful a.c.-traction locomotives for coal-train service in Wyoming, USA.

● **BELOW**
The carbody-style locomotive, popular in the 1940s and 1950s, was displaced by the more versatile road-switcher type. Only a few railroads now use this older style, including LTV Mining, which has a fleet of antique EMD-made F7As.

with its U25B. The U25B road-switcher developed 2,500 hp with its 16-cylinder, 7FDL-series prime mover. Following GE's entry into the market, a horsepower race was on. To meet North American railroad's demands, EMD, GE and Alco (which has since, in 1969, ceased locomotive production) began to develop both four- and six-axle road-switcher locomotives of ever-increasing output. EMD's most popular models were: the four-axle 2,000-hp GP38, the six-axle 3,000-hp SD40 and the 20-cylinder, 3,600-hp SD45. GE peaked with the 3,600-hp U36C. Both builders dabbled in high-horsepower dual-prime mover eight-axle monsters, but this big locomotive's limited flexibility resulted in weak sales.

● DESIGN IMPROVEMENTS

The 1970s saw many electrical improvements. The 1980s brought microprocessor control. In the mid-1980s, GE introduced the DASH-8 line, a successful 4,000-hp design that put GE at the forefront of the locomotive market. In the mid-1990s, improvements in

● **RIGHT**
GE introduced the a.c. traction motor with its AC4400CW, a model that closely resembles earlier, d.c. traction locomotives. This model proved popular with Western railroads, which use them mainly to haul heavy mineral-trains in the mountains.

SD45-DIESEL-ELECTRIC	
Dates produced	1965–71
Builder	General Motors (Electro-Motive Division)
Engine	20 cylinder 645 cc per cylinder
Power	3,600 hp

microprocessors enabled both builders successfully to apply a.c. traction motor technology to North American freight locomotives. This was the most significant improvement to American locomotive design since the advent of the diesel-electric. By using a.c. traction, locomotive builders were able to improve dramatically the tractive effort of a single locomotive. In 1996, the first 6,000 hp a.c. traction locomotives were being tested and sales of 4,000–5,000 hp a.c. locomotives dominated the new locomotive market.

● **ABOVE**
In 1996, the Union Pacific Railroad (UPR) took delivery of EMD's latest a.c.-traction locomotives, the "upgradeable" SD90MAC. These locomotives have a 4,000 hp prime mover and can accept a 6,000 hp prime mover that is being developed.

● **RIGHT**
A new EMD SD75M, featuring a safety cab and colourful warbonnet paint-work, rests between runs at Corith Yard, Chicago, Illinois. Despite a trend towards a.c. traction motors, the Santa Fe Railroad has remained committed to the traditional d.c. motor.

AMERICAN SHORT LINES

American short-line railroads are those smaller carriers that operate fewer than 350 route miles (560 km) and produce revenue of less than $40 million.

● MANY NEW SHORT LINES

Since the mid-1970s, many new short-line railroads have been formed. These new lines are mainly branch and secondary main lines disposed of by larger railroads in recent downsizing. Traditionally, healthy short lines had a choice of buying secondhand locomotives from larger railroads or new ones from builders. Through the mid-1970s, builders offered a variety of low and medium horsepower, switchers, road-switchers and specialty diesel-electric locomotives that appealed to short-line needs.

● EMD SWITCHERS AND "GEEPS"

General Motors (Electro-Motive Division), the main builder of new locomotives, offered a line of switcher-type engines featuring a short wheelbase that were popular with both short lines and larger railroads for use in yards and on secondary track. This range began with the 600 hp SC and SW locomotives

● TOP
New Hampshire & Vermont (NHV) Railroad operates on several branch lines formerly operated by Boston & Maine and Maine Central. It uses Alco RS-11s and EMD GP9s. NHV RS-11 switchers are pictured at Whitefield, New Hampshire.

● BELOW
Green Mountain Railroad (GMR) runs freight- and passenger-trains in Vermont. Usually, EMD's GP9s handle freight-trains and its Alco RS-1 road-switcher is used on passenger-trains.

● ABOVE
Many American short lines operate with obscure locomotives. Massachusetts Central railroad has a rare EMD NW5, one of only 13 built. This 1,000 hp road-switcher was originally owned by Southern Railway.

CENTURY-425	
Dates produced	1964–6
Builder	American Locomotive Company (Alco)
Engine	251C
Gauge	4 ft 8½ in
Power	2,500 hp
Capacity	16 cylinders

in 1936 and ended with the 1,500 hp
SW1500 and MP15 in the mid-1980s.
Another EMD locomotive popular with
short lines was the GP series commonly
known as "Geeps", particularly the
lower-horsepower, non-turbo-charged
1,500 hp GP7, 1,750 hp GP9 and
2,000 hp GP38.

● SHORT LINES PRICED OUT OF NEW LOCOMOTIVES

As the price of new locomotives began to
climb, more short-line railroads began to
buy used and remanufactured locomotives.
Also, as the large railroads disposed of
branches, they had less need for the types
of locomotives required for branch-line
service, glutting the used market with
switchers and "Geeps". By the late 1970s,
few short lines were placing orders for
new locomotives; instead, they operated
with hand-me-downs. As a result, short
lines are operating with a great variety of
old, secondhand locomotives, long
discarded from main-line service. As a

group, short lines feature the greatest
diversity of locomotives in the USA.
Locomotives built by Alco, which ceased
production in 1969, and many other
curious and obscure models can be found
working on short lines around the USA.

● LEFT
In the 1970s, the
Santa Fe railroad
converted many of its
EMD-made F7 cab-
units to road-
switchers designed as
CF7s. The
Massachusetts Central
Railroad bought one
CF7 from Santa Fe in
1984. The CF7 has
been popular with
short lines looking for
secondhand
locomotives.

● ABOVE
Sierra Railroad was one of the last short lines
to use Baldwin locomotives regularly. To
operate its 80 km (50 mile) railroad, it owned
several Baldwin S-12 diesel-electrics. Many
short lines held on to Baldwins long after
larger railroads discarded them.

● LEFT
New Hampshire &
Vermont GP9 No.
669 switchers at
Whitefield, New
Hampshire. NHV,
like many modern
short lines, operates
"first-generation"
diesels – those that
replaced steam
locomotives – on
lines let go by larger
railroads.

AMERICAN PASSENGER TRAINS

The diesel-electric made its passenger début in 1934 with the Burlington Northern railroad's Pioneer Zephyr and Union Pacific Railroad's M-10000 City of Salina.

● PIONEER ZEPHYR INTRODUCES THE PASSENGER DIESEL

After World War II, American railroads began ordering diesel-electrics in quantity for general passenger service. As with the freight market, the General Motors Electro-Motive Division (EMD)

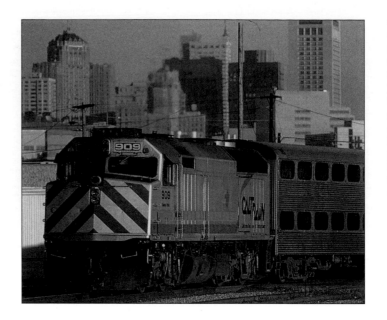

● LEFT
Cal-Train operates commuter-rail services between San Francisco, San Jose and Gilroy, California. The agency uses EMD's 3,000-hp F40PH locomotives in push-pull mode. The locomotives always face outbound (south).

FL9 DIESEL-ELECTRIC/ELECTRIC	
Dates produced	1956–60
Builder	General Motors (Electro-motive Division)
Engine	20 cylinders 567C or 567D1
Power	1,750 hp or 1,800 hp
Capacity	567 cc per cylinder

dominated the market for new passenger-locomotives. Its most popular models were its E series, streamlined locomotives featuring twin 567 prime movers and A1A trucks. Each truck had three axles but the centre axle was not powered. The E7, rated at 2,000 hp, was introduced in 1945; the E9, rated at 2,400 hp, was introduced in 1954 and remained in production until 1963. While other builders also produced passenger locomotives – notably Alco with its PA series – none was particularly successful in the USA. The PA was well liked by enthusiasts for its superior aesthetics but generally disliked by railroads for poor performance and high maintenance.

EMD also made four-axle F Series locomotives for passenger service. Western railroads preferred F units, mainly because of their pulling ability in heavily graded territory.

Beginning in 1956, the New Haven Railroad (NHR) took delivery of FL9s (dual-mode diesel-electric/electric) from EMD for use in electrified territory around New York City. These versatile locomotives use a diesel engine or electric third rail.

● THE AGE OF AMTRAK

Amtrak, America's National Railroad Passenger Corporation, an American government-owned body set up in 1970,

Amtrak maintains several dual-mode FL9 diesel-electric/ electric locomotives for service between New York City and Albany, New York. The now-defunct New Haven Railroad (NHR) ordered 60 of these specialty locomotives between 1956–60.

● OPPOSITE
Amtrak locomotives in Chicago, Illinois, await assignment. On the left, No. 828 is a General Electric AMD-103. On the right are EMD-made F40PHs.

● **RIGHT**
In the Northeast Corridor – between
Washington, DC and New Haven, Connecticut
– Amtrak operates AEM7 electrics in a high-
speed service up to 130 mph.

assumed responsibility for most intercity
passenger runs in 1971. By the 1980s,
governmental operating agencies relieved
most railroads of commuter-train
responsibilities. A new generation of
motive power was developed for Amtrak
and the commuter lines. In the early
1970s, EMD made a passenger version of
its successful SD40 freight-locomotive,
but the six-axle passenger SDP40Fs, with
full cowl hood, proved largely
unsatisfactory for passenger service.
Many were later sold to the Santa Fe
railroad for fast freight service. In 1976,
EMD introduced the F40PH, a turbo-
charged 3,000 hp, four-axle locomotive
well received by Amtrak and the
commuter lines. Several hundred were
sold in the USA and Canada. Meanwhile,
General Electric offered its six-axle
3,000 hp P30CH, with limited success.

● **ELECTRICS AND TURBOLINERS**
Amtrak's Northeast Corridor is mostly
electrified. In the 1970s, General Electric
made about 30 E60 electrics to replace
40-year-old former Pennsylvania Railroad

● **LEFT**
Two General
Electric Genesis
AMD-103s lead
Amtrak's California
Zephyr westbound
at La Grange,
Illinois.

GG1 electrics operating on that route. In
the early 1980s, EMD licensed the Rc4
electric locomotive from the Swedish
company Allmänna Svenska Elektriska
Aktiebolaget (ASEA), and from that
design made more than 60 high-hp
AEM7 electrics for high-speed service on
the Northeast Corridor.

Amtrak has had limited success with
articulated turboliners. In the mid-
1970s, it placed seven streamlined Rohr
Turboliners in service in its Empire
Corridor, between New York City and
Niagara Falls. Each set has a 1,140 hp
power-car at both ends.

● **THE NEXT GENERATION**
In the early 1990s, Amtrak began taking
delivery of several new types of locomotives. It received about 20 utilitarian-
looking 3,200 hp DASH-8 32PBs from
General Electric, followed by several
varieties of GE's Genesis Locomotive.
The Genesis is a semi-streamlined
product that uses a monocoque
(frameless) body and a GE prime mover.
Amtrak and commuter-operator Metro-
North also use dual-mode Genesis
locomotives for service in the third-rail
electrified territory around New York
City. On its Californian routes, Amtrak
uses EMD's F59PHIs, streamlined
passenger locomotives exhibiting what
EMD deems the "swoopy look".

AMERICAN METRO-ELEVATED LINES

Traditional elevated lines, using steel structures to carry electrified rapid-transit tracks above city streets, can still be found in New York City, Philadelphia and Chicago.

● TRADITIONAL ELEVATED LINES

All of these elevated lines are operated in conjunction with a subway/heavy-rail metro system. In New York and Philadelphia, use of elevated lines is restricted to outside the central, commerical area – downtown. This leaves Chicago as the only remaining American city with a traditional elevated rapid-transit structure at its centre. Its skyscrapers and antique route present an incongruous mix of architecture.

In the mid-1980s, Boston, Massachusetts, replaced most of its Orange Line elevated structure with a

● RIGHT
New York City Transit Authority's logo.

● LEFT
An outbound D train heads towards Coney Island, Brooklyn, Long Island, New York City, in a frigid December in 1993. The New York City Transit Authority (NYCTA) has several thousand rapid-transit cars in its fleet and operates the most extensive rapid-transit system in North America.

● LEFT
An inbound train from Flushing, Queens, New York City, heads for Times Square, Manhattan, in 1993. This is one of many elevated lines operating in the borough of Queens.

● ABOVE
Chicago's famous "Loop" is the last traditional elevated rapid-transit line to operate in the heart of an American city. A set of Morrison-Knudsen cars negotiates the "Loop" on 4 July 1995.

modern metro-rail system, leaving the Lechmere-North Station section of Green Line Light-Rail route as the only significant elevated structure in the area.

● MODERN HEAVY METRO-RAIL TRANSIT

Some American metropolitan areas that did not have traditional elevated lines are today served by modern heavy-rail metro transit systems. Like the traditional elevated lines, these systems use electrically powered multiple-unit transit vehicles (usually powered by third rail) on a variety of gradient-separated right-of-ways – underground (subway), in open cuts or on concrete elevated structures. The most extensive modern systems are the Washington D.C. Metro and, serving the greater San Francisco metro area, the Bay Area Rapid Transit, known as BART.

CHICAGO TRANSIT AUTHORITY (CTA) SERIES 2000 CARS

Date produced	1964
Builder	Pullman Car & Manufacturing Company
Weight	47,400 lb
Propulsion	General Electric
Seating	47/51 seats

● RAPID TRANSIT CARS

New York City and Chicago operate the largest rapid-transit fleets in the USA. In recent years, New York has modernized its rolling stock with new cars from north American builders such as Bombardier, and by having its older cars rebuilt. In the late 1980s and early 1990s, many of New York City Transit cars were built by MK Rail in the former Erie Railroad shops at Hornell in rural western New York state.

New York, with its new and rebuilt cars, has successfully eliminated the colourful graffiti that covered most of its fleet in the 1970s and 1980s. Its cars' spray paint-resistant surfaces are now nearly graffiti-proof.

Chicago's fleet of cars represents a host of different builders. Following discontinuation of streetcar service in the 1950s, Chicago rebuilt most of its large fleet of President Conference Committee (PCC) streetcars for rapid-transit service on elevated and subway lines. In 1964, Chicago took delivery of 180 new cars from Pullman. In 1969, it ordered 75 new stainless-steel cars from the Budd Co. In the 1970s, Chicago took delivery of 200 cars from Boeing-Vertol and another 600 cars from Budd. Chicago's most recent order was in the early 1990s, for 256 cars from Morrison-Knudsen.

● **ABOVE**
Into the 1950s, New York City operated a fleet of antique open-platform cars on one remaining Brooklyn elevated route, the Myrtle Avenue Line.

● **ABOVE LEFT**
On Independence Day 1995, in Chicago, Illinois, a red, white and blue set of cars made by Boeing-Vertol heads south on the Howard Street line.

● **BELOW**
Chicago has one of the largest networks of traditional elevated-metro rail lines. A 3200 Series car made by Morrison-Knudsen heads downtown on the Howard Street Line.

AMERICAN LIGHT RAIL

In the mid-1970s, San Francisco, California, and Boston, Massachusetts, ordered new light-rail vehicles to replace worn President Conference Committee cars (PCCs). This represented the first orders for new cars in several decades and began to reverse a long decline in American light-raise use.

● AMERICAN LIGHT RAIL REVIVAL

The new cars, built by Boeing-Vertol, had design flaws. There were no further orders for them. By the mid-1990s, fewer than 20 years after most of the Boeings were delivered, both cities were buying replacements.

● CANADIAN LEAD FOLLOWED BY SAN DIEGO

The real light-rail revival came in 1978 at Edmonton, Alberta, Canada, when the city inaugurated its 4½ mile (7 km) line. This was the first all-new light rail system in recent memory. The system used 14 six-axle Siemens-Duewag U2 light-rail vehicles (LRVs). The USA followed Canada's lead in 1980 when the San Diego Trolley (SDT) began operating in California. Like the Edmonton system,

MASSACHUSETTS BAY TRANSPORTATION AUTHORITY (BOSTON) TYPE 7	
Dates produced	1986–8
Builder	Kinki Sharyo
Client	MBTA (Boston)
Voltage	600 kV d.c.
Axles	Six
Weight	84,800 lb
Propulsion	Westinghouse
Seating	50 seats

● ABOVE
San Francisco's brightly painted, rebuilt PCCs have proved popular with tourists. The cars were regauged to operate on the San Francisco Municipal Railway's light-rail lines. Usually, the PCCs are assigned to the F-Market line, which does not use the Muni-Metro subway. This car is painted to represent Boston's MBTA scheme of the 1950s.

● OPPOSITE BOTTOM
An LRV made by Kawasaki, Japan, negotiates the broad-gauge single-track Media Line at Media, Pennsylvania, in suburban Philadelphia, in 1992. Philadelphia was the only city to buy these non-articulated cars.

● BELOW
A Type 7 car built by Kinki Sharyo of Japan prepares to turn at Cleveland Circle in Boston, Massachusetts, in 1993. Boston uses three different kinds of LRVs on its system.

● LEFT
Boston's Massachusetts Bay Transportation Authority (MBTA) bought
100 Boeing-Vertol light-rail vehicles (LRVs) for its Green Line Light-Rail
routes. The Mattapan-Ashmont High-Speed Line, part of the Red Line,
still uses older President Conference Committee (PCC) cars.

● SAN FRANCISCO RE-EMBRACES THE PCC CAR

In 1995, San Francisco re-established its long-dormant F-Market line, using rebuilt PCC cars from Philadelphia, Pennsylvania. The cars were completely overhauled by M-K Rail, a division of Morrison-Knudsen, at Hornell, New York, and regauged for San Francisco tracks. To celebrate the PCC design, each car was painted differently, using traditional liveries from American cities that had formerly operated this traditional type of streetcar. The idea made this one of the most colourful fleets of regularly operated streetcars in the USA. San Francisco's once large fleet of PCC cars were mostly retired by the mid-1980s when new Boeing-Vertol cars arrived.

Some American cities have started a trend using low-floor cars. Portland, Oregon, was the first US city to use them, taking delivery of 46 Type-2 cars from Siemens Transportation Systems in 1993.

the SDT line, running from the commercial centre to the Mexican border at San Ysidro, was an entirely new light-rail system and also used six-axle U2 cars, painted bright red. The SDT system proved popular. Extensions and new routes have since been built.

● VARIETIES OF LIGHT-RAIL VEHICLES

Since then, nearly a dozen new light-rail systems have started operating. The latest is in Dallas, Texas, which started operating in June 1996. Its 18 km (11 mile) system uses yellow-and-white cars built by Kinki Sharyo/Itochu International.

LRVs used in the USA have few uniform standards and even the gauge varies somewhat. Most cities use the standard 4 ft 8½ in gauge, but New Orleans in Louisiana and Philadelphia and Pittsburg in Pennsylvania use 5 ft 2¼ in and 5 ft 2½ in.

Many builders' cars are in service. They range from traditional American companies, such as Perley Thomas with vintage streetcars built in 1923–4, used in New Orleans, to Bombardier which built cars for Portland, Oregon's light-rail system, and also include many foreign companies such as Italy's Breda and Japan's Kinki Sharyo.

● LEFT
Sacramento, California, the original terminus of the transcontinental railroad, began operating its new light-rail system in 1987. Trains of four-coupled Siemens-Duewag U2A LRVs regularly traverse the streets of the Californian capital.

TOURIST LINES IN AMERICA

In the past 20 years, dozens of railroads have begun operating tourist-trains. Some of these lines are strictly passenger-carriers, often catering to specialty markets such as luxury dinner-trains.

● **POPULARITY OF TOURIST LINES**

Other tourist trains are short-line railroads looking to supplement freight revenue. The type of motive power used on these lines varies greatly but tends towards the historic, to appeal to the travelling public. Some lines use steam-locomotives, others vintage diesel-electrics. Many lines that use diesels paint them in elaborate schemes reminiscent of the schemes used in the 1940s and 1950s.

● **CALIFORNIA'S NAPA VALLEY WINE TRAIN**

Napa Valley Wine Train is one of the most successful operations. It runs several trips a day through the Napa Valley and caters for up-market patrons. Guests have dinner and wine-tasting aboard vintage heavyweight passenger cars hauled by FPA-4 diesel-electronics

● **LEFT**
The Green Mountain Railroad (GMR) operates its freight- and passenger-trains with a fleet of well-maintained historic locomotives. In 1993, EMD's GP9 1850 leads a freight up the gradient at Ludlow, Vermont. The GP9 was popular in freight and passenger service.

● **LEFT**
The East Broad Top Railroad (EBTR) in central Pennsylvania offers an authentic railroad experience. It uses vintage equipment appropriate for its line. It has four operational 36 in gauge Baldwin Mikados. No. 15 is pictured at Rockhill Furnace.

● **BELOW**
In 1989, the Boone Scenic Railway (BSR) took delivery of a brand-new JS Class Chinese-made Mikado, seen here atop the railroad's high bridge, north of Boone, Iowa. The brightly painted steam locomotive is popular with train-riders.

made by Montreal Locomotive Works (MLW), Alco's Canadian subsidiary. Four of these engines, acquired from the Canadian passenger-rail authority Via Rail, entered service in 1989. They have a burgundy-and-gold paint scheme that reflects the colours of California's wine country. Several tourist lines acquired FPA-4s from Via Rail when it upgraded its locomotive fleet and disposed of many of these older models.

● **GREEN MOUNTAIN RAILROAD**

The Green Mountain Railroad (GMR), a successful short line in rural Vermont, USA, has augmented freight revenue by operating a seasonal excursion-train. For this service it maintains a vintage Alco RS-1 diesel – the precise model used by its predecessor Rutland Railway in passenger service in the 1940s and 1950s. It also uses General Motors Electro-Motive's GP9s when passenger-

FPA-A	
Dates produced	1958–9
Builder	Montreal Locomotive Works (MLW) (Alco)
Engine	251B
Power	1,800 hp
Capacity	12 cylinders

trains are heavily patronized, particularly in autumn when the coloured foliage attracts hundreds of riders daily.

● **NEW STEAM PROVES POPULAR**

The Boone Scenic Railroad (BSR) operating a former interurban line in central Iowa, USA, has taken a novel approach towards passenger-trains. In 1989, it took delivery of a brand-new JS Class Chinese-made Mikado. Several other American tourist lines have also ordered new steam locomotives. For Boone, which derives all its revenue from excursion-trains, the new steam locomotive has been a great success. Other tourist lines operate with traditional American-built steam locomotives restored for tourist service.

● **ABOVE LEFT**

A Northern Pacific Railroad (NPR) Ten-Wheeler 4-6-0, Class S-10 328, leads a passenger-excursion train across Wisconsin Central's St Croix River bridge in Wisconsin. This Alco-built locomotive 1907 is the only remaining NPR 4-6-0.

● **RIGHT**

In autumn 1989, the Napa Valley Wine Train began dinner-train service in the scenic Californian valley. Four streamlined Via Rail, FPA-4 locomotives provide power. They were bought from the Canadian passenger transport authority.

CANADIAN FREIGHT TRAINS

Canadian railroads had a more conservative approach to motive power than had their American counterparts. Canadians preferred tested, established locomotive models rather than innovative ones and continued to rely on steam locomotives through the 1950s.

● THE 1950S

While Canadian railroads' transition to diesel-electrics copied the USA, they began serious conversion to diesel later and were far less experimental in choice of models. In the late 1950s and 1960s Canadian Pacific and Canadian National began taking delivery of mass-quantities of essentially stock American diesel-electric designs. General Motors Diesel Ltd (GMD) and Montreal Locomotives Works (MLW), Alco's Canadian subsidiary, were the main builders. Baldwin and Fairbanks-Morse also marketed their products in Canada.

Canadian railroads bought a few streamlined F units but largely dieselized freight operations with road-switcher-

● BELOW
Two Ontario Northland RS-3s await assignment. These MLW-built engines are almost identical to RS-3s built in the USA by MLW's parent, Alco.

type locomotives had a solid market with Canadian Pacific and Canadian National. Both railroads acquired many MLW S-Series switchers.

● CANADIAN LOCOMOTIVES TAKE ON A DISTINCTIVE LOOK

In the late 1950s, Canadian locomotives took on a distinctive appearance, distinguishing them from their American counterparts. Mechanically, they were the same. For example, Canada bought MLW's 1,800 hp RS-18 that featured a slightly different hood-style from Alco's RS-11 preferred by American railroads. The locomotives were identical in most other respects. MLW continued to make diesels after Alco discontinued American production in 1969. Through the 1970s, MLW built distinctive Canadian locomotives

based on Alco designs. In 1979, Bombardier acquired MLW and continued to build locomotives into the mid-1980s. It has since left the new locomotive market.

● **CANADIAN SAFETY-CABS**

In the early 1970s, safety-conscious Canadians began ordering road-switcher hood-unit locomotives with full-width, four-window "Canadian safety-cabs", or "comfort cabs". These reinforced cabs were designed to protect the crew in derailments or collisions. Canadian railroads also began equipping locomotives with "ditch-lights", bright headlamps near the rail, for increased visibility. For many years, these were trademarks of Canadian motive power. American lines have since emulated Canadian practice and safety-cabs and ditch-lights are now standard features on North American locomotives.

● **BELOW**
The wide-nosed "Canadian safety-cab", or comfort cab, and ditch-lights were once trade-marks of Canadian National locomotives. Now they are standard features on most North American freight locomotives. Here, a quartet of CN GP40-2s with comfort cabs leads a northbound freight.

● **LEFT**
Canadian National (CN) acquired SD701 locomotives from General Motors in 1995. In 1996, CN began to receive its first SD751s, part of an order for more than 300.

● **THE 1990S**

In the mid-1990s, Canadian National and Canadian Pacific began ordering what were essentially stock locomotives from GM and GE, although some assembly was done in Canada. In 1995, Canadian Pacific ordered a fleet of GE AC4400CWs for heavyfreight service in the Canadian Rockies. While Canadian Pacific had experimented with a.c. traction, this investment represented the first commerical application of the new technology in Canada. Meanwhile, Canadian National has remained firmly committed to traditional d.c.-traction motors. Instead of trying a.c. locomotives, it ordered more than 300 General Motors six-axle SD701 and SD751 locomotives.

RS-18	
Dates produced	1956-68
Builder	Montreal Locomotive Works (MLW) (Alco)
Engine	12-cylinder, 251B
Power	1,800 hp

● **OPPOSITE**
A Canadian Pacific (CP) MLW RS-18 switches at St Martin's Junction, Quebec, in 1993. The Canadian-built RS-18 was not significantly different from the American-built RS-11.

CANADIAN PASSENGER TRAINS

Steam locomotives were used in passenger service in Canada until the early 1960s.

● 1950S TO 1980S

In the 1950s, Canadian National and Canadian Pacific began acquiring passenger-diesels. Both railroads used Canadian-built General Motors Diesel (GMD) FP7s. FP9s and passenger-equipped road-switchers. These loco-motives were in most respects the same as

FPA-A	
Dates produced	1958–9
Builder	Montreal Locomotive Works (MLW) (Alco)
Engine	12-cylinder, 251B
Power	1,800 hp

● **LEFT**
Via Rail, the Canadian passenger-train operating agency, ran a fleet of Montreal Loco-motive Works FPA-4s inherited from Canadian National. Four FPA-4s at Central Station, Montreal, Quebec, in 1984.

● **BELOW LEFT**
Via Rail's LRC loco-motives did not always haul the specially designed tilting LRC train sets. In 1985, an LRC locomotive leads a conventional train in Toronto, Ontario.

● **BELOW**
Toronto's GO Transit was an early user of push-pull commuter train sets. On the end opposite the locomotive is an auxiliary cab. This provides head-end power in addition to comfort for the engineer. Some of GO Transit's auxili-ary cabs were built from old F-units.

their American counterparts. Canadian National also used FPA-2s and FPA-4s, the MLW passenger version of Alco's FA freight locomotives. The E unit, popular in the USA, did not catch on in Canada, although Canadian Pacific owned a few.

● TORONTO COMMUTER OPERATIONS

In 1966, Toronto's commuter agency GO Transit ordered specially built road-switchers from General Motors, called GP40TCs, for its passenger runs. The GP40TC is essentially a modified version of the 3,000-hp GP40 freight loco-motive, equipped with a headend power generator to operate electric heat and lights on passenger cars.

GO Transit was an early proponent of push-pull commuter trains. Rather than run traditional trains with the locomotive always on the front, GO Transit equipped the rear of its trains with auxiliary power-cabs. The auxiliary cabs, built from the shells of old F-units, provide head-end power and comfortable operating cabs. By using an aux-cab, GO Transit obviated need for a specially equipped locomotive to provide head-end power.

● LIGHT, RAPID, COMFORTABLE

The Canadian passenger agency Via Rail took on the operation of most long-distance passenger-trains in 1997. Looking for a better way to haul passengers, it decided to acquire modern "tilt" trains. Between 1981–4 Via Rail took delivery of LRC trains, powered by 31 specially designed locomotives built by Bombardier's Montreal Locomotive Works. The LRC locomotives proved problematic and are no longer made.

● ABOVE LEFT
Canadian National box-cab electrics lead a commuter-train at Val Royal Station, Montreal. CN's suburban commuter service to Deux Montagnes, Quebec, uses overhead electrifi-cation. The traditional electrification and electric locomotives, some nearly 80 years old, were replaced in 1995 with a modern system.

● ABOVE RIGHT
In the late 1980s, Via Rail began replacing its ageing carbody-style locomotives with new F40PHs from General Motors.

● BELOW
Ontario Northland Railroad operated its Northlander passenger-train with FP7m loco-motives and secondhand Trans-European Express articulated train sets acquired in 1977.

Canadian Light Rail

Canada's three main light-rail systems are in Calgary and Edmonton, in Alberta, and in Toronto, Ontario. Both the Alberta systems were built new in the late 1970s and early 1980s. The Toronto system evolved from a traditional street-car system.

Toronto and Montreal both operate underground electrified metro-rail systems. The Montreal system uses an unusual rubber-tyre propulsion. Vancouver, British Columbia, features an elevated metro-rail system called Sky-Train, which uses computer-controlled unmanned cars operating from a 600 volt d.c. third rail.

EDMONTON'S U12 LIGHT RAIL VEHICLES (LRVS)

Dates produced	1978–83
Builder	Siemens-Duewag
Voltage	600 volts d.c.
Axles	Six
Weight	71,585 lb
Propulsion	Siemens
Seating	64 seats

● EDMONTON

Edmonton inaugurated its 7 km (4½ mile) line in 1978. By 1992, the system had expanded to 10.6 km (6½ miles). In the 1900s, Edmonton operated a streetcar system. This was discontinued after World War I, in favour of highway transportation. Edmonton's light-rail system began operations with 14 six-axle articulated Siemens-Duewag U2 light-rail vehicles (LRVs).

● CALGARY

Calgary followed Edmonton's lead and opened its 12 km (7½ mile) all-new light-rail line in 1981. By 1992, Calgary's

In the 1960s, Toronto still operated venerable Peter Witt cars, which seem particularly antique compared to a modern CLRV.

● OPPOSITE
Toronto operates 196 four-axle CLRV cars built between 1977–82. A TTC car pauses at Dundas Avenue, Toronto, in 1985.

● BELOW
Toronto once boasted a large fleet of President Conference Committee (PCC) cars. In the past two decades, most were replaced with CLRVs.

system was operating more than 27 km (17 miles), with extensions planned. Calgary operates a fleet of more than 80 six-axle articulated Siemans-Duewag U2 cars. It has also operated two experimental U2 cars that feature a.c.-traction motors. Most North American light-rail systems use traditional d.c.-traction motor technology. In the USA, the Baltimore, Maryland, light-rail system also uses a.c. traction.

● TORONTO
Toronto relied on a large fleet of President Conference Committee cars (PCC)s. In 1977, the city began replacing traditional PCCs with new Canadian Light Rail Vehicles (CLRVs). By the early 1990s, Toronto was operating nearly 100 four-axle single-unit CLRVs and more than 50 six-axle articulated CLRVs. Like cities in the USA, Toronto was looking at low-floor cars for future operation.

CUBA'S RAILWAY NETWORK

Cuba has an almost unbelievable diversity of classic American steam locomotives, left suspended in time following Fidel Castro's revolution in 1959.

Some of them came from former lines in the USA and their builders' plates read like a who's who of American locomotive history: H.K. Porter, Rogers, Davenport, Alco, Vulcan Ironworks and Baldwin. Small wonder that over the past ten years Cuba has become a focus for steam lovers worldwide, as traditional outposts of steam in Eastern Europe, South Africa and India have declined.

All of Cuba's steam-locomotive fleet work on the island's vast sugar plantations but, in the course of work, often

● **BELOW**
At the Boris Luis Santa Coloma mill network on Cuba, the flat crossing at Robles has a classic American signal-box on stilts. A Baldwin Mogul built in January 1920 completes the picture.

● **RIGHT**
A German-builder's plate on a Cuban locomotive.

travel over the national railway system's main lines. Far from being the small locomotives found on many of the world's sugar plantations, Cuba's engines are, in many cases, fully fledged main-liners and typical of the engines that many American roads were operating in the early years of this century.

A remarkable variety of gauges exists on Cuba, too, including standard, 3 ft, 2 ft 10½ in, 2 ft 6 in and 2 ft 3¾ in.

A remarkable number of centenarian engines is active, including Baldwins of 1878, 1882, 1891, 1892 and 1895, and a pair of Rogers of 1894.

Cuba looks likely to remain reliant on steam locomotives for many years to come, one of the most exciting bastions of classic steam power into the new century.

● **RIGHT**
This Mogul, built by
H.K. Porter in 1919,
was pictured
trundling a yellow
caboose, that is
guard's van, across
the rails of the Carlos
Manuel de Cespedes
sugar mill in
Camaguey Province,
Cuba.

● **FAR RIGHT**
The wreckage of
Baldwin 2-8-0
No. 1542 Manuel
Fajardo at Obdulio
Morales sugar mill's
locomotive shed in
Sancti Spiritus
Province, near the
spot where its boiler
exploded. The boiler,
wasted at the front
tube-plate, had been
welded. The result
was disastrous. The
driver, oiling the
motion, was blown to
pieces and only his
legs were found. The
fireman, in the cab,
was thrown about
15 m (50 ft) across
the depot yard.

4-4-0 WESTINGHOUSE	
Builder	Baldwins, New York, USA
Client	Havana Central Railroad
Gauge	4 ft 8½ in
Type	4-4-0
Driving wheels	5 ft 8 in
Capacity	Cylinders 18 x 24 in
Weight	119,600 lb

● **OPPOSITE**
Baldwin-built 2-8-0 No. 1390 eases a rake of
freshly cut sugar cane down the Arroyo Blanco
line at the Rafael Freyre sugar mill in Holguin
Province, Cuba.

● **ABOVE**
Cuba has several Fireless engines. This huge
0-4-0, built by Baldwin in September 1917,
works at the Bolivia sugar mill, in Camaguey
Province.

● **ABOVE**
Cuba has no coal reserves, so the island's
locomotives are oilfired. The cab interior of a
Baldwin 2-8-0 raising steam at the E.G.
Lavandero sugar mill.

SOUTH AMERICAN STEAM

● BELOW RIGHT
One of the Teresa Cristina's Texas 2-10-4s bursts out of Sideropolis Tunnel on the Rio Florita branch line. The engine, No. 313, was built by Baldwin in 1940.

South America was a major area of importance during the worldwide decline of steam from the 1950s and remained so until the mid-1980s.

The area is fascinating because of its diversity of locomotive types, operating terrain and gauge.

● ARGENTINA AND URUGUAY

Argentina displayed the British school of design. It had more locomotives than any other South American country – about 1,000 active as late as the mid-1970s. Five gauges operated over 80 different locomotive types. One of the world's most exciting steam lines is Argentina's 75 cm (2 ft 6 in) gauge Rio Gallegos, a

● ABOVE
A 4-8-0 15B Class of Argentine Railways. Britain's Vulcan Foundry exported 30 of these two-cylinder engines to Argentina in 1949. Mixed-traffic engines, they gained distinction in hauling seasonal fruit over the 1,200 km (750 mile) run from the Rio Negro Valley to Buenos Aires, working 1,000-ton loads on passenger-train timings.

● LEFT
In the 1950s, the Yorkshire Engine Co. of Sheffield sent two Moguls to Paraguay. The engines have a distinct LMS air about them as shown in this picture of No. 152 Asunción in the shed yard at San Salvador.

coal-carrying line 52 degrees south, near the Strait of Magellan. This route operates 2-10-2s, hauling 1,800-ton coal-trains, and is one of the steam sights of the world.

Uruguay, across the River Plate from Buenos Aires, was another stronghold of classic British designs, rivalling India in faithfulness to the domestic product.

● BRAZIL

Brazil has long been a land of discovery for rare and unrecorded locomotive types, because of its vast terrain and the relative remoteness of much of the country. Brazil's best-known steam-line is the metre-gauge Doña Teresa Cristina in the south-east where the world's last Texas Type 2-10-4s work. Formerly, they worked across the Mato Grosso, the highlands in eastern Mato Grosso state. These giants of American steam superpower, scaled down to metre-gauge operations, contrast with a plethora of sugar-plantation systems in the area around Campos, north of Rio de Janeiro, and in the north-eastern state of

● **ABOVE**
Texas Type 2-10-4s and Mikado 2-8-2s in the shed yard at Tubarao on Brazil's metre-gauge Doña Teresa Cristina Railway in south-east Santa Catarina Province.

● **BELOW RIGHT**
Brazil's Doña Teresa Cristina Railway acquired 6 metre gauge 2-6-6-2 Mallets from Baldwin between 1941–9. They were introduced for the heavily graded, curving route from Tubarao to Lauro Muller.

Pernambuco behind the Atlantic Ocean port and state capital Recife (formerly Pernambuco). These sugar usinas hosted a fascinating variety of metre-gauge veterans, many from Brazil's former main-line railways such as the Leopoldina, Mogiana, Paulista and Sorocabana.

● **CHILE, PERU AND PARAGUAY**
Chile's waterless Atacama Desert was host to the last Kitson Meyers, weird, double-jointed beasts that bent in the middle and had a chimney at both ends. These engines were an articulated

predecessor of the more successful Garratt engine.

The Kitson Meyer's rarity was complemented by the incredible veterans found farther north in Peru where an 1870 classic American Rogers 4-4-0 was active at Puerto Eten.

The wilds of the Paraguayan Chaco were host to a fascinating stud of veterans that hauled *quebracho* from the interior to ports along the River Paraguay for conveying to the Atlantic Ocean at Buenos Aires. The logs were once a major source of tannin, used as tanning agents and in medicines. The flame-throwing woodburners of the Chaco contrasted well with the standard-gauge main line from Asunción to Encarnación with its woodburning Edwardian Moguls, from North British Glasgow and Hawthorn Leslie 2-6-2Ts.

Thus, diversity and exotica have been left over from the great age of steam. Although, by the 1990s, much of the diversity had disappeared, survivors will linger on in ever-diminishing pockets into the new century.

15B CLASS 4-8-0	
Date	1949
Builder	Vulcan Foundry, Lancashire, England
Client	Argentine Railways (Ferrocarriles Argentinos; FA)
Gauge	5 ft 6 in
Driving wheels	5 ft 8 in
Capacity	Cylinders 19 x 28 in
Total weight in full working order	154 tons

MODERN SOUTH AMERICAN LOCOMOTIVES

In the past, many South American countries had closer ties with Europe and the USA than with each other. This resulted in at least six different railway gauges being built on the continent.

● SNAKING BULK TRAFFIC IN PERU

Peru's railways climb the upper slopes of the highest Andean summits but adhesion only is used, resulting in spectacular sights as long mineral-trains snake up and around grand mountains. Diesel is the established form of motive power. Peru has more than 1,350 km (839 miles) of standard gauge and just 300 km (186 miles) of 3 ft gauge.

Peru's oil-burning steam locomotives were replaced by diesel-electrics, the most numerous being General Motors (GM) Type JJ 26 CW-2B 3,300 hp Co-Cos built by Villanes of Brazil.

● RESTRUCTURING IN CHILE

Chile has just under 2,576 km (1,600 miles) of 5 ft 6 in gauge and more than 1,600 km (1,000 miles) of metre-gauge

● ABOVE
An Alco-built 1,000-hp diesel-electric, No. 107, shunting on a multigauge track in the station yard at Mérida, Yucatan, Mexico. The locomotive belongs to the Ferrocarriles Unidos del Sureste.

● BELOW
Argentina's changing motive-power character is shown at Constitution Station, Buenos Aires. A diesel-electric stands beside a Class 8E three cylinder 2-6-4 suburban tank, one of the most successful locomotive types ever delivered to the country.

track still in use after restructuring of the railway system. The metre-gauge lines to the north of Santiago are diesel-operated but the standard-gauge Southern Railway, extending from Santiago south to Puerto Montt, an area of German settlement, has been electrified. Electric locomotives of Swiss origin are being built in Chile. Diesel has taken over the narrow-gauge routes.

ARGENTINE CLASS 8E 2-6-4T SUBURBAN	
Date	1923
Gauge	5 ft 6 in
Client	Buenos Aires & Great Southern Railway
Driving wheels	5 ft 8 in
Capacity	3 cylinders 17 x 26 in
Pressure	200 lb sq in
Axle loading	19 tons
Weight in full working order	101 tons

● BELOW
The nameplate and numberplate of one of the two Moguls delivered to Paraguay from Yorkshire Engineering Co., named Asunción after the country's capital city Nuestra Señora de la Asunción founded in 1538. The sister engine was No. 151, named Encarnación, after Encarnación de Diaz, the agricultural centre opposite Posados, Argentina, with which it is connected by ferry.

The E32 Co-Cos from GAI of Italy are Chile's most numerous passenger-electric locomotives. Most diesels are from GM in Argentina. The DT600, DT1300, DYDT5100, D7.100 and D1600 classes account for more than two-thirds of Chile's diesels. The most numerous diesel classes on the 5 ft 6 in gauge are GAIA 1350, GAIA 1050 and Alco RSD16. Metre-gauge diesels are supplied by General Electric (GE), the most numerous class being the G22CO with more than 100 units in service. The 201 km (125 miles) of electrically-operated track is entirely serviced by Russian-built locomotives.

● **DIESEL TAKE-OVER IN ARGENTINA**

Argentina has more than 22,500 km (14,000 miles) of 5 ft 6 in gauge, nearly 3,220 km (2,000 miles) of 4 ft 8½ in gauge and more than 14,500 km (9,000 miles) of other gauges. Much of the rail system radiates from Buenos Aires. Because of British influence in the early days, most equipment is British in appearance. Diesel has all but taken over, yet steam is still active on the Esquel and Rio Gallegos lines of Patagonia. On main lines, Fiat-type diesel railcars are

● ABOVE
A 2-8-0 of Mexico's Southern Pacific Lines threads a freight-train along the West Coast route, which stretches 2,104 km (1,307 miles) from Guadalajara, Mexico's second-largest city, to the border of the United Mexican States (UMS) and the USA.

● BELOW
An electric locomotive pulls a freight-train through the Argentine-Chilean Pass at Caracoles, near Socompa in Chile's Antofagasta Province.

common, although freight traffic on the many electrified lines is mainly hauled by British outline diesels. Lines carrying the heaviest commuter traffic around Buenos Aires have been electrified for many years.

● **HEMATITE, STEEL AND SÃO PAULO IMPACT ON BRAZIL**

Brazil is South America's largest and most industrial country. The two main gauges are 5 ft 3 in and metre. Bulk freight has increased and made new export routes a priority, because of vast hematite deposits, which is the chief source of iron, in Minas Gerais state, the steel industry of Volta Redonda town in Rio de Janeiro state, Brazil's first steel-making town from 1942, and the manufacturing potential of the fastest-growing city in the world, São Paulo, itself a great railway centre. Track up-grading and electrification has been in progress for the past 15 years. Diesels work the various narrow gauges and the non-electrified main lines. There are just more than 1,932 km (1,200 miles) of 5 ft 3 in gauge, 24,150 km (15,000 miles) of metre-gauge with just more than 885 km (550 miles) electrified. Freight account for 99 per cent of traffic.

EUROPEAN SHUNTERS

In the days of steam, locomotives for shunting or gravity marshalling-yard work were sometimes specifically designed but many, also, were those pensioned off from main-line duties. To an extent, this practice still applies but from the 1950s increasing attention was paid to efficiency and fitness for purpose.

● **LEFT**
Members of the numerous Swiss Federal Railways class of diesel-tractor built between 1950–68, represented by Tm" 736 at Chambrelien in 1996, are often involved with work on the permanent way.

● **SHUNTING WITHIN STATION LIMITS**

These shunters come in many shapes and sizes, depending to a degree on whether what is required is casual shunting at a relatively small station or transfer work with moderate loads on the main line from time to time.

For the lighter duties, locomotives are usually four-wheeled and range from about 50 hp to about 300 hp. Propulsion can be diesel or electric. In Switzerland, alternative power sources are provided in the same locomotive and can be selected. For example, in sidings where there is no overhead-line equipment, the diesel engine provides power to the electric-traction motors. Some are fitted for remote radio control, enabling the driver to operate from the lineside, thereby performing the role of the traditional shunter. Small machines can be driven by people without the lengthy, rigorous training needed for a main-line driver, and, when not driving, they perform other station work.

Larger locomotives tend to be six-wheeled or Bo-Bo, diesel or electric. Diesel is usually preferred for its flexibility.

● **MARSHALLING YARDS AND TRIP FREIGHTS**

The bulk of marshalling-yard and trip-freight work is done by Bo-Bos where the prime power source is a diesel motor or overhead electric supply often giving an output of more than 1,000 hp. At gravity marshalling yards, standard locomotives with special low gearing for propelling wagons over the hump are sometimes used. In more recent years, some gravity-yard shunters have been fitted with radio to permit operation from the control tower. Other specialist shunters include a normal locomotive semi-permanently

● **LEFT**
Berne-Loetschberg-Simplon (BLS) No. 401 at Spiez, near Interlaken, Bern Canton, Switzerland, in 1988, with its notable jackshaft drive. These locomotives are similar to shunters on Swiss Federal Railways, Schweizerische Bundesbahnen (SBB), and to others in Sweden. Their power coupled with a reasonable turn of speed enables them to work trip-freights and to act as carriage-shunters.

● RIGHT
● RIGHT
The trend to make small shunters more versatile is increasing. They have been fitted, for example, with radio control. A new application is accumulators, fitted to this electric-shunter of Switzerland's Spiez-Erlenbach-Zweisimmen Railway so that it can work in non-electrified sidings. Tea 245.021 is at Zweisimmen in 1995.

● BELOW
This Deutsche Reichsbahn Class 101 No. 512, almost the classic small diesel-shunter, acts as carriage-shunter at Riesa, Dresden, Germany, in 1991. It was later No.311.512 on the unified German railway system (DBAG).

● RIGHT
Older main-line locomotives are downgraded to light duties, performing trip-freight and shunting work as needed. Class 1200 of Portuguese Railways – Companhia dos Caminhos de Ferro (CP) – built by Sorefame in Portugal in 1961–64, do such work in Southern Portugal. Nos. 1213 and 1210 are pictured resting at the railway-junction town of Tunes, Algarve, in 1996.

ELECTRIC SHUNTER: BERN-LOETSCHBERG-SIMPLON RAILWAY (BLS)

Date	1943
Builders	mechanical: Swiss Locomotive and Machine Works (SLM) electrical: SA des Ateliers de Sécheron
Gauge	1,435 mm
Class	Ee 3/3
Axle (wheel) arrangement	030 (Whyte notation 0-6-0)
Catenary voltage	a.c. 15 kV, 16.7 Hz.
Weight in working order	38 tonnes
Rating	One hour, 462 kW (about 619 hp)
Maximum service speed	40 kph

coupled to a similar power-unit without cab or related console. Such units are sometimes called "cow and calf".

Larger, non-specialized shunters can work "trip freights" between their own yard and others in the vicinity, or to factory sidings.

● **LARGE PASSENGER STATIONS**
At most large passenger stations, the "station pilot", often in gleaming condition, is a familiar sight as it deals with empty stock or remarshals trains. The locomotives are often members of the same class, or a variant of those found in marshalling yards. Sometimes the only difference is the fitting of extra, or different, braking equipment or couplings.

● ABOVE
Hungarian State Railways (MAV) has a sizeable class of modern Bo-Bo electrics built by Ganz Mavag from 1983 onward. Their 820 kW (1,100 hp) enables them to cover a wide range of duties, including carriage pilot, heavyfreight shunting and trip-freights. No. V46. 054 is pictured at the river-port of Szeged (Szegedin), on Hungary's border with then Yugoslavia, in 1993.

EUROPEAN FREIGHT

Reconstruction of Europe after World War II and growing international trade brought a huge resurgence in rail freight. This traffic had to be integrated with equally large volumes of passenger-trains and so locomotives had to be able both to handle heavy loads and to run at relatively high speeds.

Carriage of many classes of freight by rail has steadily declined. New business, however, is arriving as road-freight tractors and trailers are transported by rail across national boundaries, sometimes with drivers accommodated in sleeping-cars on the train. Intermodal traffic, with either swap-bodies or vehicles designed to operate on rail or road, is not a new concept but it is being further developed. The transport of standard-gauge wagons on special metre-gauge bogies or transporter-wagons continues to cut the cost of time delays and trans-shipment, especially in Switzerland.

● **ELECTRIC LOCOMOTIVES**
As the mixed-traffic locomotive's development progressed along similar lines, the superficial appearance of the

● LEFT
A new country and new livery have brought a striking change to former Deutsche Reichsbahn Class 242, which was bought by Lokoop, a Swiss consortium, and hired out. The engine, working on the Swiss Südostbahn in 1996, is pictured at Schindellegi in a livery advertising transport to a nearby mountain resort.

motive power on each rail system varied normally only to the extent of front-end body shape and the ventilation grilles' style and position.

Most adopted the Bo-Bo formation. In countries where heavy trains tackle steep gradients, however, locomotives with the Co-Co arrangement were introduced. In more recent years, developments in multiple working and remote radio control have enabled the use of two or more compatible locomotives at the head and a locomotive cut into the train. This is, among other things, to relieve weight on the drawbar between the locomotive and the train's

● ABOVE
Class 140 of German Railways (DBAG) was devised as a freight version of a similar passenger-class. It first appeared in 1957, and to 1973 nearly 900 were built. They handle anything from empty-carriage workings to medium-tonnage freights. No. 140 009-2 is pictured at Murneau, south of Munich, Bavaria, in 1994.

● LEFT
In sharp contrast to the bustle of the French scene, a freight-train in southern Portugal waits to leave the junction station of Tunes, Algarve, headed by Alco-built A1A-A1A diesel-electric No. 1503 in 1996.

● RIGHT

Two locomotives look excessive for this light freight-train at Venlo, Limburg Province, in the Netherlands in 1989, but Netherlands Railways-NV Nederlandse Spoorwegen (NS)-diesel-electric No. 6401, built in 1955, is part of the train that is in the charge of NS 2213. It is ironic that it is hauling a member of the class destined to lead to its withdrawal.

FRENCH STATE RAILWAYS (SNCF) CLASS BB 22200

Date	1976
Builder	Alsthom/MTE
Gauge	1,435 mm
Axle arrangement	BB
Catenary voltage	d.c. 1,500 v, a.c. 25 kV single phase (dual voltage)
Wheel diameter	1,250 mm
Weight in working order	89 tonnes
Rating	4,360 kW
Maximum service speed	160 kph

front vehicles. Longer trains also improve line capacity and therefore economic performance of the line.

● DIESEL LOCOMOTIVES

Diesel power, with locomotives working in multiple on heavy trains, is the only practical course on non-electrified lines or where traffic is lighter. The available tractive effort is generally lower than electric locomotives, but continuing use of diesels widely throughout Europe can be foreseen because of the flexibility of operation coupled with, usually, a mixed-traffic availability and, in some cases, lighter axleloading.

● BUILDERS

All the larger and some of the smaller countries of mainland Europe have the capacity to build both diesel and electric locomotives. However, the case now is that few builders design, manufacture and erect a complete locomotive. Credit for the design or manufacture of a particular class of locomotives often goes to the company or works which does the final erection. In practice, the design may well be that of the erecting company but components – bodies, motors, electrical equipment and other items – are likely to have been provided by other locomotive manufacturers.

● LEFT
French National Railways (SNCF) BB22288 Louhans leaves the extensive marshalling yards of Villeneuve-St Georges, south-eastern Paris, with a long train of empty car-transporters in 1996.

EUROPEAN RACK RAILWAYS

Rack railways are specially built to climb steep gradients in mountainous areas.

● TOURIST LINES

Most but not all tourist lines exist to convey skiers in winter and walkers, or just sightseers, in summer high into mountains. Other lines enable the tourist to reach points from which spectacular views can be obtained.

Track gauge varies from 800 mm to standard gauge. Propulsion is generally by an electric power-car pushing a control-trailer up the grade but the touristic value of the steam locomotive has not been lost on some operators who, in recent years, have ordered new steam locomotives using oilfiring and needing only one man in the cab. For obvious reasons, the track of each is relatively short. Examples of both types of line are illustrated.

● **LEFT**
Austria's metre-gauge Achenseebahn uses both Riggenbach rack-and-pinion and adhesion to climb from Jenbach, in Austria in Tirol, east of Innsbruck, to the lake that gives the railway its name. The locomotives date from 1899. No. 2 and its vintage coaches are pictured leaving Jenbach in 1980.

● **LEFT**
Switzerland's 800 mm gauge Brienzer-Rothorn Bahn, between Brienz, on Lake Brienz in Bern Canton, and Rothorn, has put into service three new steam locomotives of revolutionary design but conventional external appearance. These are oilfired and can be operated by one man. The first, No. 12, was delivered in 1992 and is pictured at Brienz in 1995.

● **BELOW LEFT**
The Monte Generoso Railway has been operated successively by steam, diesel and from 1982 electricity. The train is pictured having just arrived at the summit station, which was being modernized in 1989.

ELECTRIC RAILCAR – MONTE GENEROSO RAILWAY

Date	1982
Builder	Swiss Locomotive and Machine Works (SLM)
Client	Monte Generoso Railway
Gauge	800 mm Abt Rack
Class	Bhe 4/8
Axle arrangement	Four of the eight axles of the two-car unit are driven
Catenary voltage	d.c. 650 v
Weight in working order	34.1 tonnes
Rating	810 kW (about 1,086 hp)
Maximum service speed	14 kph

● **LEFT**
A popular mountain line in Austria is the metre-gauge Schneebergbahn, south of Vienna, from Puchberg to the summit at Hochschneeberg. No. 999.02 of Austrian Federal Railways dating from 1893, pauses at Baumgarten in 1986 before tackling the next stage of the climb.

● **BELOW LEFT**
The oldest locomotives on the standard-gauge Erzberg line of Austrian Federal Railways (ÖBB) were Class 97, first in service in 1890.

● **BELOW RIGHT**
Not all rack railways are in mountains. In Hungary, Budapest has an important standard-gauge line that partly serves commuters but is mainly for citizens wishing to reach the hills behind Buda, the old Magyar capital on the west bank of the River Danube. The line was originally steam-worked but Switzerland's SLM works provided the stock when the line was electrified in 1929. Car 55 is pictured leaving the lower terminus in August 1993.

● **CONVENTIONAL RAILWAYS WITH RACK AID**

The main aim of conventional railways with track assistance is to provide communication between towns and villages for passengers and freight conveyance. Often, tourist areas are served as well. Indeed, if this were not so, the viability of many lines often operating in relatively sparsely populated regions would be at risk.

The track gauge is generally metre and the trains appear at first sight quite conventional with an electric-locomotive hauling a moderately long train of coaches. Other trains might be hauled by single or double electric power-cars, in effect locomotives with passenger or baggage accommodation in the body. If track configuration permits, speeds of more than 75 kph are achieved over the adhesion sections but on rack sections about less than half of that can be expected.

● **INDUSTRIAL LINES**

A most spectacular example of industrial lines was the "Iron Mountain" railway from Vordernberg, in the Styria, Austria, to Eisenerz. Of standard gauge, there were some passenger services but its main purpose was to bring iron ore from Eisenerz, a mountain consisting almost entirely of iron ore, to a huge iron and steel works at Donawitz, west of Leoben in Styria. Steam was the motive power until the last few years of its existence when specially fitted diesel locomotives joined a rack locomotive purpose-built for the line. These achieved only a modest degree of success. Passenger traffic declined to the point where it could be handled by a single four-wheel, rack-fitted diesel-railcar.

This Austrian Federal Railways – Österreichische Bundesbahnen (ÖBB) – line closed in 1986 because of a fall in demand for steel coupled with the fact that it was cheaper to import ore from outside Austria. The last ore-train ran under diesel power on 27 June 1986. No fewer than seven steam locomotives have been preserved. Five of them are Class 0-6-2 Ts dating from 1890, the most popular with the crews, and one of which stands on a plinth in the town square. One is a 0-12-0T and one a 2-12-2T, built in Germany in 1941 and now standing on a plinth at Vordernmarkt Station.

EUROPEAN DMUs

The diesel multiple unit (DMU), the most flexible of all means of rail passenger transport, is used in Europe on all gauges and in many configurations.

● SINGLE RAILCARS

Single railcars range from a unit capable of coupling to another power-unit, to a control-trailer or just to a freight-wagon or passenger-coach. Operating alone, a single railcar can often be sufficient to maintain the passenger traffic on a narrow-gauge line, such as the Austrian Federal Railways 760 mm gauge line linking the Neider-Österreich (NÖ) towns of Gmünd and Gross Gerungs in the Greinerwald, or standard-gauge routes like the picturesque cross-border route between the Austrian Tirol town of Reutte and the German resort and winter sports centre Garmisch-Partenkirchen in the foothills of the Bavarian Alps.

● ABOVE
Netherlands Railways (NS) diesel-electric Class DE IIs were built by Allan, in 1953 and extensively rebuilt in 1975–82 by NS. This unit had just arrived at Arnhem, in Gelderland Province, in 1989.

● BELOW
The modern appearance of this rebuilt X4300 Series unit of French National Railways (SNCF) belies the fact that the class was introduced in 1963. In 1988, a typical representative, from Dinant, Belgium, awaits its return working at Givet, in the Ardennes Department of north-eastern France, near the border with Belgium.

The ability to strengthen the train quickly, to cope with known or sudden peaks of traffic, by adding a powered vehicle to run in multiple without reducing its line speed, is invaluable on services which share, for part of the route, the tracks of a main line where lengthy track-occupation by slow trains is unacceptable. Such units are capable of 120 kph.

On branch lines or secondary routes with a relatively infrequent service, any cut in speed from hauling unpowered trailers is not serious. However, many modern trailing-vehicles offer relatively

● **RIGHT**
In Bavaria, German Railways No. 614-012 pictured about to leave Hersbruck and head south for Nuremberg in 1985. These sets have self-tilting suspensions.

GERMAN FEDERAL RAILWAYS (DBAG) CLASS 614

Date	1971
Builder	Orenstein & Koppel/Uerdingen
Client	DB
Gauge	1,435 mm
Class	614 three-car set
Power unit	One MAN diesel-engine in each power-car, driving all wheels on one bogie via hydraulic transmission
Weight in working order	123 tonnes total (all three cars)
Rating	670 kW
Maximum service speed	140 kph

● **ABOVE**
Coachwork made by Budd of USA seems popular with Portuguese Railways for its DMUs. These sets dating from 1989 work Rápidos – expresses stopping at main stations – as well as local trains. One curves away from the railway junction of Tunes, Algarve, in 1996.

little resistance, so speeds can be relatively high, an important factor where the bus is the potential rival for traffic.

● **UNITS OF TWO OR MORE CARS**
The duties of units of two or more cars can range from branch-line work through local passenger to semifast and, in some cases, high-speed intercity services.

At the lower end of the speed-and-capacity scale are two-car sets in which only one vehicle is powered. At the other end of the scale are sets with two power-cars between which run one or more trailers.

These units are usually used on standard-gauge lines but also run with medium-distance semifast traffic on local and branch-line services. Recent developments in Germany with two-car tilting sets were sufficiently successful for

progress to be made to a further class having suspension of Italy's Pendolino type, with a maximum authorized speed of 160 kph. Their value has been particularly appreciated on lines such as the Bavarian one from Nuremberg to Hof, which suffers from stretches of frequent curvature. There, tilting trains can be permitted higher speeds than trains with conventional suspension.

● **BELOW**
Austrian Federal Railways (ÖBB) have revolutionized speed and comfort on lesser-used lines with modern Class 5047 railcars built from 1987 onward. Passenger-loads have risen as a result. No. 5047-028 a backdrop of mountains at Reutte-im-Tirol in 1994.

EUROPEAN EMU

The electric multiple unit (EMU) dates back to the turn of the century. In its simplest form, d.c. motors were controlled by robust mechanical tap changers made for relatively low maintenance costs, which balanced the high cost of line power supply. A bonus was that units could be coupled electrically and driven by one person. The main attraction, however, was probably that turnround times at terminuses were significantly cut because no locomotive change was required.

Operators of underground railways and metros found the system attractive not least because, in the restricted environment, a d.c. electric supply could be provided relatively cheaply by third rail.

This simple system saw few dramatic changes until the 1950s when the development of electronics and hi-tech engineering transformed the scene in nearly every aspect of EMU design and construction.

● THE MODERN EMU – LOCAL AND INTERMEDIATE TRAFFIC

In mainland Europe, the Netherlands can probably claim the most concentrated

● **ABOVE**
In contrast with the angular design of recent years, this Austrian Federal Railways two-car EMU epitomized the flowing lines adopted by several European countries from the 1950s. No. 4030.309, one of a batch built by Simmering-Graz-Pauker between 1956–9, is pictured about to leave St Margrethen, Switzerland, for a cross-border run into Austria's Vorarlberg Province, to Bregenz on Lake Constance in 1994.

● **BELOW**
These units, readily strengthened by adding trailers, set a standard for the modern thyristor-controlled EMU able to handle suburban and regional services equally well. They are used throughout Switzerland's Federal railway network. Similar versions have been bought by private railways. A unit is pictured arriving at Lausanne's main station in 1993. A French Train Grande Vitesse (TGV) – a high-speed train – and a former Swiss TEE unit now in grey livery are present.

use of EMUs. Few lines are not electrified and the proximity of towns and villages in this densely populated land calls for trains with high-capacity seating and good acceleration and braking.

In 1975, the Netherlands railways coined the term "Sprinter" for a two-car unit. Two- and three-car variants soon followed. The name was quickly copied by British Rail. In Belgium and around the big cities of France, Germany and Italy the EMU is important. The Swiss Federal Railway briefly flirted with EMUs in the 1920s, some of which are still used on departmental duties, but moved from locomotive haulage of short-distance trains to sophisticated EMUs from the mid-1950s. The latest units can be formed of two power-cars with up to three intermediate trailers and are termed Neue Pendel Zug (NPZ). Variants can be seen on the private railways where, in many instances, they form the backbone of the fleets. Thyristor control is well established following the usual difficulties experienced in many countries with development models. Reliability is now such that many of the numerous metre-gauge systems operate power-cars with similar technology.

Austria boasts a similar and sizeable class of attractive three-car sets built between 1978 and 1987 for suburban and middle-distance work.

NEUE PENDEL ZUG (NPZ) – SWISS FEDERAL RAILWAYS

Date	Four prototypes, 1984. Production, 1987-90
Builders	Mechanical: Flug und Fahrzeugwerke AG, Altenrhein, Switzerland; Schweizerische Locomotiv und Maschinenfabrik (SLM), Winterthur, Switzerland; Schindler Waggon AG, Pratteln, near Basel (Basle), Switzerland Electrical: A.G. Brown-Boveri & Cie, Baden, Baden-Württemberg, Germany
Gauge	1,435 mm
Class	RBDe4/4 (now Class 532)
Axle arrangement	All four axles driven on each power-car
Catenary voltage	a.c. 15 kV, 16.7 Hz
Weight in working order	70 tonnes (including driving-trailer)
One hour rating	1,650 kW (about 2,212 hp)
Maximum service speed	140 kph

● THE MODERN EMU – EXPRESS SERVICES

Few genuine EMUs have been designed specifically for long-distance express-services, but in 1965 Austria Federal Railways introduced a class of six-car sets with a permitted speed of 150 kph. All included a dining-car for some of the most prestigious services, including the run between Zurich in Switzerland and Vienna. No longer in the forefront of express travel, they have been refurbished and are usefully employed on expresses over the Semmering Pass.

● ABOVE

The Netherlands has long gone its own way with design. To some, Plan ZO/Z1 (ICM 1/2) "Koploper" three-car units are ugly. However, they are practical: the door beneath the driver's raised cab enables passengers to have unobstructed gangway-access to all vehicles.

● ABOVE RIGHT

The rounded outline of the 1950s is carried through in this four-car EMU of Trafik AB Grängesberg-Oxelosund Jarnvag, a Swedish private railway operating west of Stockholm. It is standing at Katrineholm in 1981. The X20 Class was built in 1956–7. It was ahead of its time, because the power-car is in the train rather than being a motored driving-vehicle.

● RIGHT

The Austrian 4020 Class EMU is similar in appearance to the Swiss NPZ but differs in technology. Between 1978–87, 120 units were built. They have proved most successful in S-Bahn and medium-distance work alike and were built by Simmering-Graz-Pauker, with electrical parts by Brown-Boveri, Elin and Siemens. Four traction motors produce 1,200 kW, about 1,608 hp, for each three-car unit, to permit a 120-kph service speed. No. 4020-116 sits beneath mountains at St Anton in 1990.

EUROPEAN DIESEL — MAIN-LINE

● BELOW
Diesel locomotive No. 232-231 stands, in 1992, at Brandenburg, former residence of Prussia's rulers, now in Lower Saxony, on a double-deck shuttle train to Potsdam. Brandenburg and Potsdam are respectively 60 km (37 miles) and 27 km (17 miles) south-west of Berlin.

Main-line diesels began to become prominent in the 1950s as steam started to decline. Some countries had seen at first hand diesels operated by the American Army just after World War II. The first large diesels were modelled on American lines. In some cases, virtual copies were made under licence or using imported components. One look at a large Belgian diesel shows from whence came the inspiration. Other examples were in Scandinavia where the Nohab Company of Trollhättan, Sweden, set a style that, externally at least, showed a transatlantic influence, which spread even to countries in the then Eastern Bloc.

The diesel's field of operation was almost universal for freight-trains. Some classes are geared specifically for this work. In passenger service, they tended to work on secondary lines or main lines that could not justify electrification costs. The locomotives can be classified by transmission type.

● ELECTRICAL TRANSMISSION

Electrical transmission is the more popular. A diesel-engine drives a generator to power electric-traction motors. The system is relatively simple,

robust and easy to maintain. Proponents of hydraulic transmission, however, claim less precise control and lower efficiency.

The 5100 Class Co-Co of Belgium's national railways, the Société Nationale des Chemins de Fer Belges (SNCB), is powered by an engine producing 1,580 kW (about 2,118 hp) at 650 rpm built by Cockerill/Baldwin and has a 120-kph service speed. Germany, however, is where one of the most popular and sturdy classes of diesel-electrics is in

widespread use. It originated at the October Revolution Locomotive Works in Lugansk (Voroshilovgrad, 1939–91), Ukraine, part of the former USSR. A batch of Co-Co locomotives, now Class 230, was built in 1970 for what was then the Deutsche Reichsbahn (DR) of East Germany. Another batch, Class 231, arrived in 1972–73. A final batch of 709 locomotives was delivered between 1973–82. With a massive diesel engine delivering 2,950 hp and a 120 kph top

● ABOVE
This diesel-electric of the Grand Duchy of Luxembourg's railways, the Société Nationale des Chemins de Fer Luxembourgeois (CFL), was built by Brissonneau & Lotz, of Aytre, in 1958. In 1995, standing at Esch/Alzette, in Luxembourg, at the border with France, it shows clear signs of French origin. Its duties include heavy trip-freights in Luxembourg's industrial south.

● ABOVE
The Austrian Federal Railways (ÖBB) Class 2043 and similar Class 2143 are, at 1,100 kW or 1,475 hp, of modest power by European standards. Yet they are the most powerful locomotives in Austria and find work on several non-electrified secondary lines.

DEUTSCHE REICHSBAHN CLASS 132

Date	1973
Builder	October Revolution Locomotive Works, Voroshilovgrad (Lugansk), USSR
Gauge	1,435 mm
Class	132 (now 232 on DBAG, unified German railways)
Axle arrangement	Co-Co
Weight in working order	123 tonnes
Rating	2,200 kw (appox 2950 hp)
Maximum service speed	120 kph

speed, they proved ideal for passenger and freight use.

With the reunification of Germany in 1990, their diagrams gradually spread across the country with favourable comment from drivers of the Deutsche Bundesbahn (DB), operating in what was the former West Germany. An uprated version, Class 234, has a 140 kph top speed. Many of the locomotives are being re-engined and appear to have a long life ahead.

Diesel-electrics have great importance to smaller nations where heavy traffic between major sites of population and commerce is offset by the need, on social if not economic grounds, to provide services over lightly laid secondary routes. An example is Portugal whose machines range from 117 tonne Co-Cos rated at nearly 3,000 hp to modest 64 tonne Bo-Bos producing about 1,300 hp.

● HYDRAULIC TRANSMISSION

The Deutsche Bundesbahn, now German Federal Railways (DBAG), favoured, for its large diesels, hydraulic transmission made by Voith, of Heindenheim, Brenz. This works like automatic gearboxes in cars. Between 1968–79, four classes of Bo-Bo machines were built, culminating in Class 217. Of this, there are two types. One is fitted with the Pielstick 16 PA 4V 200 engine producing 3,000 hp and a 140 kph top speed. Their weight in working order is 78.5 tonnes, compared with the Class 234's 123 tonnes.

Austrian Federal Railways (ÖBB) also favours Voith transmission in its relatively small 1,475 hp machines whose work is decreasing as lines are electrified.

● **ABOVE**
German Federal Railways (DBAG) Class 218 is the last in a long line of locomotives of similar appearance, 500 being built in 1968–79. The most powerful of these Bo-Bo diesel-hydraulics is rated at 2,061 kW, about 3,000 hp. Nos. 218.905 and 908, rebuilds from Class 210, are pictured at Brunswick, Lower Saxony, in 1991.

● **RIGHT**
The unmistakable French lineage of this Portuguese Railways Class 2601 stands out in 1996 as a diesel-electric Bo-Bo built by Alsthom passes Santa Clara, in Beira Litoral Province, south-west of Coimbra, Portugal's former capital.

EUROPEAN MAIN-LINE ELECTRICS

World War II left mainland Europe's railways heavily damaged. Many administrations could see that electrification was the way forward but a neutral country, Switzerland, led the way.

● SWITZERLAND TURNS TO HYDRO-ELECTRIC POWER

Switzerland has no natural resources for power apart from abundant water. In the war, coal for steam-engines was practically unobtainable, so engineers

turned to the source already harnessed, hydroelectric power (HEP). The country had used electric locomotives and railcars for many years but there was now a need for powerful, relatively fast mixed-traffic machines with a high power weight ratio and good adhesion. This pointed to providing motors on all axles.

In 1944 it was the Bern-Loetschberg-Simplon (BLS) railway that set the trend. It did so with a small class of eight Bo-Bo locomotives weighing only 80 tonnes, having four, fully suspended, single-phase

motors driving all four axles. Current at 15 kV, 16⅔ Hz from overhead-line equipment enabled the locomotive to operate at an hourly rating of 3,238 kW.

● UNIFIED GERMAN SYSTEM

West Germany's large, efficient fleet of steam locomotives operated into the 1970s on main-line duties but here, too, Bo-Bo locomotives of similar dimensions to the BLS machine were introduced, Class 110 in 1956 for mixed-traffic work and Class 140 in 1957 mainly for freight

● **ABOVE**
SNCF Class BB2600 dual-voltage "Sybic" 26053 heads an express-train.

● **TOP RIGHT**
A Deutsche Bundesbahn Class 120 is waiting to leave Munich Main Railway Station, Bavaria, in 1989 at the head of a train of Netherlands Railways double-deck coaches then on trial. A prototype batch of five of these advanced-design locomotives with three-phase motors entered revenue service in 1979. The production batch did not come on stream until 1987. These 60 machines have a one-hour rating of 6,300 kW, about 8,445 hp, and a maximum service speed of 200 kph.

● **RIGHT**
In 1995, a direct descendant of the trend-setting Bern-Loetschberg-Simplon (BLS) railway Bo-Bo of 1944 stands at Interlaken West Station at the head of the Thunersee from Berlin. It is one of a class of 35. With an hourly rating of 4,990 kW, about 6,690 hp, it has a maximum service speed of 140 kph.

● **LEFT**
Deutsche Bundesbahn (DB) 11 081-6 heads north out of historic Boppard, in the Rhine Valley south of Koblenz. This class of 227 locomotives is an improved version of the prolific Class 110.

but often seen on passenger-trains. Several hundred of these and variants are working in western Germany. In eastern Germany, a class was developed using thyristor control. This went into batch-production in 1982, proving so successful that it is widely used across the unified German system – the DBAG – as Class 143. The locos weigh 82 tonnes and have a one-hour rating of 3,720 kW.

● **FRANCE USES DUAL VOLTAGE**

In France, development after the war was different, not least because the various constituents of the system that had finally embraced all the main railways in 1938, the Société Nationale des Chemins de Fer Français (SNCF), had, where electrification had been tried, used noncompatible traction current. No classes of locomotive had been made in large numbers although several small batches established a development line, which might be said to lead to the impressive BB26000 Class, the Sybic, an acronym for "Systeme Bi-courant". These dual-voltage machines operate either on 1500 V d.c. or 25 kV single-phase a.c. They went into service in 1988 and gradually proved themselves. They are so successful that their numbers are increasing rapidly towards a projected target of more than 300 units. They weigh 91 tonnes, have a rating of 6,400 kW and are authorized to travel at 200 kph.

France's Trains Grande Vitesse (TGVs) – high-speed multiple unit trains – reach high speeds. The SNCF holds an official electric-traction record for on 28 March 1955 Co-Co, 1,500 V d.c. locomotive CC 7107 achieved 330.9 kph (205.6 mph) with a 100-tonne load. Next day, this record was equalled by Bo-Bo 9004 with an 81-tonne train.

● **RIGHT**
Until 1988, the French National Railways (SNCF) CC 6500 Class of 1500 V d.c. locomotive was its most powerful along with dual-voltage subclass CC 21000. They are fitted with mono-motor-bogies, enabling the gear ratio to be changed easily. At high-speed setting, maximum speed is 200 kph. They are rated at 5,900 kW, just more than 7,900 hp. CC 6563, in low-gear mode is pictured near the large marshalling yards at Villeneuve-St-Georges, Paris, in 1996.

● **LEFT**
The need to produce a modern main-line electric locomotive to cope not only with express-traffic on level ground but also with heavy gradients in Austria's mountainous regions, led Austrian Federal Railways (ÖBB) to buy a batch of ten thyristor-controlled locomotives of the Swedish Railways Class Rc2 in 1971. Class 1044 was quickly developed by the railway authorities and introduced into service in 1974. No. 1044-092, pictured at Jenbach, in Tirol, east of Innsbruck, is one of the batch with a 160-kph service speed and a one-hour rating of 5,300 kW, just more than 7,100 hp. A later version has a 200 kph service maximum. One machine is approved for 220 kph.

● **AUSTRIAN AND HUNGARIAN DESIGNS**

Austria, so often challenging in steam design with the Gölsdorf locomotives and the Giesl ejector, has a most successful Bo-Bo Class 1044 that owes something to an earlier maid of all work, Class 1042, but also to the Swedish Rc2.

Hungary, too, has the numerous Class V43. This leans on German technology, in that the first small batch was built by Krupp, of Essen, Germany. Ganz, a world-renowned locomotive works, in which Hunslet of Britain has a financial interest, is keeping pace with modern locomotive technology.

● **SWITZERLAND'S LOK LEADS FIELD**

Switzerland, however, is again leading the field with a very "hi-tech" design developed by the Swiss Locomotive and Machine Works (SLM) of Winterthur. Known as Lok 2000, the technological advances are so many that a small book would be needed to do it justice. A notable feature is its quietness when running. Swiss Federal Railways Schweizerische Bundesbahnen (SBB/CFF/FFS) know it as Class Re 460. The BLS has a variant — and the most powerful version — Class 465. A broad-gauge variant is in service on Finland's railway system. Examples have run trials in other countries.

The machines entered service on the federal railways in 1991, generally performing well. Teething troubles, however, slowed the progress of their introduction into general service. With problems solved, the class of 119 locomotives is operating widely throughout the country.

● **RIGHT**
The Netherlands, a relatively small country, has an extensive railway network, part of which is in the European international system. Class 1600 and the almost identical Class 1700 are built by Alsthom, France, based on the French National Railways (SNCF) Class BB 7200. The Class 1600s entered service in 1981, the 1700s in 1990. Capable of 200 kph, they are restricted to 160 kph. Here, in 1989, No. 1643 has just brought an express-train into the border town of Maastricht in Limburg Province.

LOK 2000

Date	1992
Builders	Mechanical: Swiss Locomotive & Machine Works (SLM), Winterthur, Switzerland Electrical: ABB Transportation Systems, Baden, Zurich, Switzerland
Client	Swiss Federal Railways
Gauge	1,435 mm
Class	Re460
Axle arrangement	Bo-Bo
Catenary voltage	15 kV
Length over buffers	18,500 mm
Weight in working order	84 tonnes
Number of traction motors	Four
Rating	1,100 kw (8180 hp)
Maximum service speed	230 kph

● **RIGHT**
Lok 2000 No. 460 015-1 of Swiss Federal Railways waits at Lausanne in Vaud Canton in 1993 after bringing in an express-train from Basel.

● **LEFT**
Belgium has a dense network of lines and demands a powerful mixed-traffic locomotive able to handle anything from light "push-and-pull" trains, through freights to expresses. The Class 21, introduced in 1984, comprises 60 machines rated at 3,310 kW, about 4,437 hp, with a 160-kph maximum service speed. They were built in Belgium by La Brugeoise et Nivelles SA and are almost identical to the chopper-controlled more powerful Class 27. No. 2157 is pictured in 1992 leaving Ghent Sint Pieters Station in the East Flanders provincial capital of Ghent on its way to the depot at Dendermonde, East Flanders.

● **RIGHT**
Italy has long produced striking and seemingly unconventional designs of locomotives. In the Class 656 Bo-Bo-Bo with its articulated body, F.S. Italia has one of the most successful designs of recent years. It is based on well-tried technology for it derives from the 636 Class dating back to 1940. Provided speeds above 150 kph are not required, these loco-motives handle expresses almost anywhere in Italy. They first entered service in 1975. By 1989, 608 had been built. Here, No. E 656-469 waits to take over a train at Domodossola, in Novara Province of the Piedmont Comparti-mento, in 1996.

EUROPEAN LOCAL PASSENGER – LOCOMOTIVE-HAULED

Until the late 1960s, it was possible to enjoy the sights and sounds of steam-hauled local passenger-trains soon to be displaced by electric and diesel traction. Because of the increased use of multiple units (MUs) with their favourable weight-per-person ratio and flexibility, many local services lost the familiar locomotive at the train's head.

The locomotive remains in use on such services for two main reasons. Firstly, and more obvious, certain lines have a mixture of relatively light passenger- and freight-traffic so that both functions can be fulfilled by a locomotive.

● **"PUSH-AND-PULL" TRAINS**

Second, in heavy passenger-traffic areas, displacement of locomotives by MUs, which often hauled trains of obsolescent coaches, meant that relatively modern machines would either have to be scrapped or sold at bargain prices. One solution was to select a class of

● **ABOVE**
Extensive improvements are being made to the line as German Railways (DBAG) Class 143 228-5 runs into Belzig-bei-Potsdam, south-west of Berlin, with a rake of double-deck coaches in 1992.

SWISS FEDERAL RAILWAYS CLASS 450

Date	1989
Builders	Mechanical: Swiss Locomotive & Machine Works (SLM), Switzerland Electrical: ASEA Brown Boveri
Client	Swiss Federal Railways
Gauge	1,435 mm
Class	450
Axle arrangement	Bo-Bo
Catenary voltage	a.c. 15 kV, 16.7 Hz
Weight in working order	78 tonnes (locomotive only)
Rating	One hour, 3,200 kW (about 4,290 hp)
Maximum service speed	130 kph

● **LEFT**
Swiss Federal Railways (SBB) No. 450 067-4 on S-Bahn service at Zurich Main Station in 1994.

● **LEFT**
The striking S-Bahn livery suits this German Federal Railways (DBAG) Class 218 as it sits beneath the impressive roof of Cologne Main Station in North-Rhine Westphalia in 1986.

displaced locomotives. It was common practice on the former Deutche Reichsbahn to use electric locomotives where appropriate, and diesels elsewhere, coupled to rakes of double-deck coaches.

● **MODERN SWISS DESIGNS**

In Switzerland, in 1989, purpose-built locomotive Class Re450 was matched to three double-deck coaches, one of which was a driving-trailer. Initially, they operated in the environs of the Switzerland's largest city, Zurich. As the S-Bahn network is extended, however, they can be found far from the city. Multiple-unit working is common, and it is not unusual to see three sets coupled together. The locomotives were the first in a new era of rail technology in electrical, mechanical and body design. They were built by the Swiss Locomotive and Machine Works (SLM) and operate on 15 kV 16⅔ Hz supply. Four, three-phase, nose-suspended motors produce nearly 4,300 hp for a weight of only 78 tonnes.

locomotives with adequate power and good acceleration, refurbish them, fit remote-control equipment so they could be driven from a driving-trailer and match them to a set of high-capacity refurbished coaches. After receiving a colour scheme that matched with or blended into the livery of the MU fleet, the "new" sets were in business. Because they are driven by one person and from either end without uncoupling the locomotive, they can take their place in intensive local services.

Both diesel and electric locomotives are fitted for "push-and-pull" working. Indeed, this is now a feature of express services, too. Another advantage is that replacement is simple, if the locomotive requires maintenance.

A good example of such working can be found in Germany's industrial Ruhr and around Cologne in North-Rhine Westphalia. However, the reason the local "push-and-pull" working was adopted in other areas and countries was not because a use had to be found for

● **ABOVE**
Diesel-electric Co-Co No. 5105 of Belgian National Railways (SNCB) rolls into Sint Pieters Station, Ghent, East Flanders, with a commuter train in 1992.

● **ABOVE**
French-built steeple-cab Bo-Bo electric No. 3618 of Luxembourg Railways, the Société Nationale des Chemins de Fer Luxembourgeois (CFL), runs into Esch/Alzette, Luxembourg's second city, in the south of the country, in 1995.

EUROPEAN LIGHT RAIL AND METRO

Mainland Europe had few truly light-rail systems in the early 1950s, apart from street tramways. As for electrified metros, the most famous must surely be the Paris *chemin de fer métropolitain*. The Métro, opened in 1900 – although one of the oldest in the world in Budapest, Hungary, was opened on 23 May 1896. Probably the most ornate in the world is the one in Moscow, opened in 1933. Similar rolling stock to that in Moscow can be seen in Budapest.

● LIGHT RAIL

There were many tramway systems in Europe after World War II, some of them of an interurban nature. In the combatant countries, most were

● **LEFT**
In complete contrast to the Strasbourg tram, delightful reminders of a past, more ornate period can be found in small trams still tackling the narrow streets and hills of the old city in Lisbon, the Portuguese capital.

THE "EUROTRAM" IN STRASBOURG	
Date (year into service)	1994
Builder	ABB Transportation, York, England
Client	Compagnei des Transports, Strasbourgeois, Strasbourg
Gauge	1,436 mm
Class	Eurotram
Axle arrangement	Variable
Catenary voltage	750 volt d.c. Power is fed to traction-inverters in the car
Maximum rating	38 kW (50 hp) per motor
Speed	21 kph

● **LEFT**
This tram is operating on an entirely new system in Strasbourg, France, the first 12.65 km (8 miles) of double-track having been officially opened on 26 November 1994. It runs on reserved track, in-tunnel or, as in this 1996 picture, in pedestrianized streets.

● LEFT
One of Europe's most extensive tram systems is in Budapest, Hungary. A modest underground heavy metro and a web of tram routes, some with reserved track, combine to provide an efficient, cheap means of getting around the city. Moskva tét in Buda is a focus of many tram routes. Car 4158 with its sister tram is pictured in 1993, about to start its Route 61 run.

damaged, some badly. Trams were put back on the streets as quickly as possible because they were and are one of the most efficient means of moving many people fast, especially in heavily populated areas.

Numerous old vehicles survived for many years until recovering manufacturing industries were able to supply the demand for new and more efficient vehicles. Smaller towns tended to replace trams with buses, particularly in France. Others turned to trolley-buses and various experimental schemes were tried, including guided buses and even Mag-lev. In Germany, the Langen-type suspended railway between Barmen and Elberfeld in Wuppertal, an industrial city in North-Rhine Westphalia, not only survived but continues to operate with comfortable modern double-cars.

Probably two tram builders made the most impact on the postwar scene, Duewag of Germany and CKD, of Prague (Praha), Czech Republic, with Tatra cars. Both produced robust reliable vehicles, which are widely used in many countries.

More recently, demand for easier access to public-transport vehicles has led to the development of sophisticated low-floor cars, some incorporating elegant and advanced bogie designs allowing low floors throughout the vehicle. General advances in control equipment used on heavy rail have readily found use on tramways.

● LEFT
Vienna is served by an expanding underground railway system. However, one of the best ways to get a feel for the city is to take the frequent trams. Routes 1 and 2 operate in opposite directions around the Ringstrasse. Standard Series E2 No. 4311, on Route 65, is pictured in 1987 standing at Karlsplatz, near the interchange with the underground.

● LEFT
Some systems fall between light-rail and heavy-metro categories. One is that in Utrecht, a bustling city and major rail junction in the Netherlands' eponymous smallest province. This unit, one of 27 built between 1981–3 by SIG of Neuhausen, Switzerland, although called a tram, operates more like a true heavy metro and has an 80-kph service speed. Here, it is pictured near Utrecht's main railway station in 1989.

● **LEFT**
Austria's private railways have for many years taken advantage of the availability of good secondhand equipment. The rolling stock waiting to leave the terminus of the Salzburger Stadtwerke Verkehrsbetriebe (SVB) near the main station in Salzburg in 1986 originated on Germany's Cologne-Bonn private railway (KBE). Today, the SVB terminus is in an underground complex, and services are operated by a fleet of light Bo-2-Bo units.

The impression of 20 years ago that the tram was noisy, rough riding and uncomfortable has changed to such an extent that suitable devices have had to be devised to warn pedestrians of their quiet approach, especially in areas restricted to public transport. Where track is well laid and maintained, the ride can be as good and often better than on heavy rail.

An ideal arrangement to take advantage of the relatively high-speed capability of the modern tram is the use of reserved track and, in some instances, redundant heavy-rail formations for part of the route. In others, light-rail vehicles are used for urban and suburban services over tracks carrying normal main-line trains such as the Swiss Federal Railway line from Geneva to La Plaine.

● **ABOVE**
The use of light-rail type vehicles on main-line tracks is spreading. Switzerland's section of line between Geneva and La Plaine is electrified at 1,500 volt d.c. for through-working to Geneva by standard French locomotives. Swiss Federal Railways have introduced these lightweight EMUs to replace time-expired main-line stock.

● **BELOW**
An EMU train on suburban service in Paris.

● **RIGHT**
The popularity of lightweight, low-floor units to replace the main-line type of construction is leading to their widening use on metre-gauge railways in Switzerland, especially where the route is substantially in an urban-style environment with frequent stops. Unit Be4/8 33 is pictured at the outer terminus of the Wynental und Suhrentalbahn line, at Menziken, south of Aarau, in 1996, about to leave for Aarau, an important station, in Aargau Canton, on the federal railways' main line from Zurich to Bern.

● **BELOW**
Another German interurban line is the Wuppertal Schwebebahn running 13.3 km (8 miles) from Oberbarmen to Vohwinkel. Its articulated cars were built from 1972–4 by MAN. They are suspended from massive girderwork dating back to the turn of the century. The route is over a river for a considerable way and elsewhere follows the course of roads.

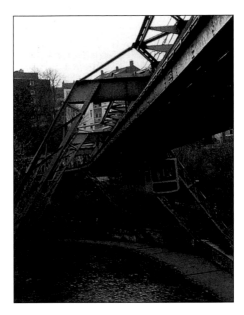

wide tunnels built by cut-and-cover method, incorporating closely spaced stations with many interchanges with other Métro lines whose tentacles spread deep into the suburbs.

Where lines emerge into daylight, they may be on viaducts or bridges spanning the River Seine, some giving fine views. The narrow multiple-unit sets in places grind around sharp curves or have to tackle steep gradients. The opportunity should not be missed to ride on one of the lines, which uses pneumatic-tyred wheels for traction and guidance, with conventional flanged wheels on rail as a fail-safe.

Using the Métro and the modern, quick RER system, which goes deep into the surrounding countryside, is the finest way to get around Paris, a remark true for all cities and conurbations that have increasingly adopted the Métro concept as a transport system for the future.

● **METRO SYSTEMS**

Such systems are generally used in large cities or densely populated conurbations, usually to provide a high-frequency, high-capacity service. In some instances, the routes are wholly or substantially in-tunnel. In other cases, tramway or heavy-rail routes have been linked or diverted to run partly in tunnel. In many instances, the term has been used on reorganized and refurbished heavy-rail routes to provide the ensuing improved services with a "brand name", a growing practice.

● **PARIS MÉTRO**

For overall utility and its mixture of retained antiquity coupled with modern technology, the Paris Métro is hard to beat. Under the streets of Paris, it has

● **ABOVE**
Germany's Oberrheinische Eisenbahn-Gesellschaft (OEG) is an example of an interurban system. It operates through four states – Bavaria, Rhineland-Palatinate, Baden-Württemberg and Hesse. It has 61 km (38 miles) of metre-gauge routes from the spa town of Dürkheim, through the commercial and manufacturing cities of Ludwigshafen am Rhein and Mannheim to Heidelberg. Trains run in or alongside roads, in pedestrianized areas and on the reserved tracks. Unit 109, built by Duewag of Düsseldorf and Uerdingen in 1974, stands in the station at Viernheim, a suburb of Mannheim, in 1986.

INTERNATIONAL EUROPEAN SERVICES

● **BELOW**
The latest Pendolino development is the ETR 470 Cisalpino. These dual-voltage trains are operated by an Italian-Swiss consortium. Services began in September 1996 from Milan to Basle and from Milan to Geneva. A train from Geneva to Milan is pictured snaking into Lausanne in 1996.

Initially, electrically powered international services were little different from the days of steam. Locomotives hauled their rakes of, usually, the best stock the originating country could provide, to the border-station where one locomotive was removed and another from the next country was added. This was not always easy. For example, at Venlo in Limburg Province of the Netherlands, the electrical system differs radically from that in Germany and the international platforms are provided with special wiring that can be switched to either power-supply. It was found convenient to use a diesel-shunter to attach and detach the main-line locomotive.

● **GERMANY, AUSTRIA, HUNGARY AND SWITZERLAND**

In Germany, Austria, Hungary and Switzerland there was and is little difficulty in through-working because the electrical supply is common at 15 kV a.c., 16.7 Hz. These countries share the German language, to a greater or lesser degree, so the main constraint is that of differing signal aspects and operating regulations, which can be overcome by training.

The French already had much experience because the railways, electrified from early days, used 1,500 volt d.c. and 25 kV single-phase a.c. In 1964, they plunged into the multicurrent field with a class of locomotives designed to cope with most situations. These had the capacity to work on 1,500 volt–3,000 volt d.c., 15 kV single-phase and 25 kV three-phase a.c. They were thus able to cross all their rail frontiers, although in practice they worked mainly Paris-Brussels-Amsterdam.

However, the complete unit, incorporating power-cars, came to the fore. Austrian Class 4010 six-car sets, introduced in 1965, working in multiple, operated an express-service from Zurich to Vienna, although they have been supplanted by locomotive-hauled stock because of inadequate passenger-capacity. Such units still work to Munich, Bavaria.

● **FRANCE DEVELOPS TGVs, GERMANY ICEs**

More recent developments are the French Trains Grande Vitesse (TGVs) – "high-speed trains" that have become multicurrent, running into neighbouring Belgium and Switzerland. From these have developed the Thalys, that is, TGVs running the Paris-Brussels-Amsterdam services. These in turn have given rise to an experimental unit, still under trial in 1996, specifically for Thalys but capable of much wider use.

Germany has produced the Class 401 Inter City Express (ICE) units in large quantity. Broadly, these match the TGV in performance and, like them, use proven technology. Most Swiss standard-gauge railways' common electrical system

● **ABOVE**
Germany's DBAG multicurrent Inter City Express (ICE) uses conventional technology to achieve speeds of up to 330 kph. The "Thunersee" from Interlaken is pictured leaving Olten railway junction in Switzerland, for Berlin in 1996.

Conventional technology and new high-grade track brought success for France's Train Grande Vitesse (TGV). Journey-times were revolutionized with a 300-kph top speed, as this image of a TGV Atlantique at speed shows.

● **ABOVE LEFT**
The quadricurrent development of the TGV for the Thalys services (Paris-Brussels-Amsterdam) was still under trial when this picture was taken at Paris, Gare du Nord, in June 1996. TGVs painted in Thalys red livery were still operating revenue services in November 1996.

● **BELOW RIGHT**
The ETR 450 can be regarded as the first commercially successful tilting train. "Pendolino" is an accepted nickname for the type.

enables them to run lucrative international services such as the Thunersee from Berlin to Interlaken.

Franco-British co-operation in constructing and operating cross-Channel international expresses involves yet another electrical complication on the British side – 750 volt d.c. supplied from a third rail.

● **ITALY DEVELOPS PENDOLINO**
Italy has developed the tilting train to the extent that the concept, with which

several countries have experimented for some years, has become acceptable for public service. The Pendolino, as it is called, draws heavily on pioneering work by British Railways with its Advanced Passenger Train (APT). The aim is to be able to use existing infrastructure for higher speeds by relieving passengers of gravitational forces in curves. Other technological developments have enabled speeds and ride-quality to be improved even more.

THE PENDOLINO (ETR 450)	
Date	1987
Builders	Fiat/Marelli/Ansaldo
Gauge	1,435 mm
Class	ETR 450 (Elletro Treni Rapidi 450)
Axle arrangement	1-A-A-1
Catenary voltage	d.c. 3,000 volt
Weight in working order	400 tonnes
Rating	4,700 kW (about 6,300 hp)
Maximum service speed	250 kph

THE PRESERVATION OF EUROPEAN TRAINS

At the turn of the century, enlightened railways and historians realized the importance of preserving equipment that had helped to make railways one of the most important developments the world has seen. Equipment was put either into a museum or on to a plinth, in the latter case often being damaged beyond repair. Mainland Europe has several fine museums, those at Nuremberg in Germany, Mulhouse in France, Vienna in Austria and Lucerne in Switzerland among them.

● PRESERVATION – WORKING RAILWAY MUSEUMS

Static exhibits though informative are lifeless. Private individuals' efforts were largely responsible for restoring locomotives and rolling stock to working condition. Funds were raised, often

● **RIGHT**
No. 298.51 pushing a snowplough reaches Grünberg in Oberösterreich (Austria) from Garsten on the 760 mm gauge line to Klaus.

slowly, to obtain unwanted and sometimes derelict items. On these, teams, usually of volunteers, laboured for months or years to achieve their aims. These were often either to run locomotives and carriages on sections of line bought after abandonment by original owners, or to persuade main-line or other companies to allow the stock to be run from time to time over their rails. For the latter, high standards had to be met and maintained. It is a great credit to the army of

volunteers that all over Europe a pool of stock is available. However, from the 1970s onward, national railways and private companies began to realize the commercial and advertising potential of possessing and running their own nostalgic services. Locomotives emerged from static display to be restored by the companies and operated frequently in connection with line or station anniversaries.

● **RIGHT**
All three types of
motive power, visible
at Gmünd depot,
Austria, in 1987.

● **BELOW RIGHT**
Preservation
volunteers' skills are
shown in this
beautifully restored
electric-railcar of the
metre-gauge Martigny
Châtelard Railway
built in 1909 in
Switzerland.

AUSTRIAN FEDERAL RAILWAYS – ÖSTERREICHSCHE BUNDESBAHNEN (ÖBB) CLASS 16

Date	1911
Designer	Dr Karl Gölsdorf
Builder	Maschin Fabrik der Österreichisch-Ungarischen Staats-Eisenbahn Ges, Vienna
Client	Kaiserlich - Königlich - Österreichische Straatsbahrien (KKSTB)
Gauge	1,435 mm
Class	BBÖ 310 ÖBb 16
Axle (wheel) arrangement	1C2 (2-6-4)
Capacity	2 cylinders (390 x 720 mm) and 2 (630 x 720 mm). Compound
Wheel diameter	2,100 mm
Weight in working order	86 tonnes
Maximum service speed	100 kph

● **OPPOSITE**
Gölsdorf-designed No. 310.23 is pictured
being cleaned before taking part in Austrian
Railways' 150th anniversary.

● **RIGHT**
In Switzerland, a double-headed train snakes
into Filisur in 1988.

● LEFT
A Belgian stream-
lined 2B1 4-4-2 built
by Cockerill of Liege
in 1939 and a
Deutsche
Bundesbahn
No. 23.023 at
Utrecht, in the
Netherlands, in 1989.

● TOURIST RAILWAYS

Tourist railways take several forms. They range from narrow-gauge lines in pleasure-parks such as Vienna's Prater – an imperial park since the 16th century but now a public place, through lines specifically built to support tourism – to main lines and branches built for trade but which attract tourists.

Lines built with the tourist in mind are often in mountainous areas and take skiers, climbers and walkers to suitable points to start their activities as well as many passengers who ride the trains just to enjoy the view. Examples are too many

● ABOVE
In Hungary, on the Children's Railways in the hills above Budapest, a Mk 45-2002 arrives in Szenchenyi from Huvosvolgy.

● LEFT
The Flying Hamburger part-preserved unit was displayed at the Nuremberg 150th anniversary exhibition in Germany in May 1985.

● OPPOSITE
The beauty of the preservation of modern steam is epitomized by this then Czechoslovakian Railways Class 241 4-8-2 No. 498-022.

to mention in Switzerland; Austria's Achensee, Schafberg and Schneeberg; and in Germany the Drachenfels, at 320 m (1,053 ft) one of the Siebengebirge of the Westerwald, on the eastern bank of the Rhine where, according to legend, Siegfried slayed the dragon.

A group of Swiss lines illustrates railways fulfilling a general commercial need but attracting tourists. These are the metre-gauge systems of the Brig-Visp-Zermatt in Valais Canton, Furka-Oberalp in Uri Kanton and the extensive Rhaetischebahn in Graubünden Kanton, which together cover the Glacier Express route.

Finally, there are lines, usually narrow gauge, which have lost the bulk of their original passenger and freight traffic to the roads but still maintain limited

services. Examples are the railways of the Harz Mountains in central Germany, Gmünd to Gross Gerungs in Austria's Neider-Österreich Province, and the "Little Yellow Train" in the Cerdagne, France.

● **ABOVE**
In Italy, beneath France's 4,807 m (15,781 ft) high Mont Blanc, the highest mountain in the Alps, a lightweight 1C (2-6-0) with inside-cylinders and outside-valve chests, built in 1910–22, waits at Pré Saint Didier to return to Aosta, the town at the junction of the Great and Little St Bernard Passes, in Aosta Province of Piedmont Compartimento.

COMMONWEALTH OF INDEPENDENT STATES (CIS)

In 1991, the former Soviet republics of the Union of Soviet Socialist Republics (USSR), the Soviet Union, formed a loose organization called the Commonwealth of Independent States (CIS). The CIS inherited more than 151,000 km of railways (94,000 route-miles) of 5 ft and more than 2,400 km of narrow-gauge railway. The narrow gauge is mostly 2 ft 6 in, with a small amount of metre- and 2-ft gauge. In addition, there are

● **LEFT**
A Class CS4T electro-locomotive stands on shed awaiting repair.

CLASS P36 4-8-4

Date	1954
Builder	Kolomna Locomotive Works, Russia
Client	Russian State Railways
Driving wheels	6 ft 0^3/$_4$ in
Capacity	Cylinders 22–22^5/$_8$ x 31 in
Boiler pressure	213 lb per sq in

61,000 km (38,000 miles) of light industrial railways within the former Soviet Union.

The industrial, mineral, agricultural and forestry lines were not subject to state railway motive-power policy and stayed with steam rather longer, especially where waste from sawmills afforded a ready supply of fuel. TO-4, TO-6A and TO7 diesels have taken over where this cheap supply of fuel is not available.

● **WORLD RECORDS**
Freight traffic dominates rail operations with the 2,000,000 ton-miles produced annually being more than the rest of the world's rail traffic put together. The L Class 2-10-0 built after World War II has been an outstandingly successful goods-engine. More than 5,000 have been built. The L Class 2-10-0s followed the successful E series 0-10-0s, some 14,000 of which were produced in slightly

● **LEFT**
S2D 4-8-4 P36 No. 0250 train No. 1 Russia in Skovorodino (formerly Rukhlovo), a town in the Amur Oblast (administrative division) of Soviet Russia, on the Trans-Siberian Railway for which it is a junction. It connects with the Amur River, 56 km (35 miles) south, on the Sino-Soviet frontier.

● LEFT
A Russian EA Class 2-10-0 locomotive stands at Manzhouli, in the Inner Mongolian Autonomous Region, just inside China's border with Russia, across from the Russian railhead, a terminus of the Trans-Siberian Railway (TSR), at Zabaikalsk. Manzhouli is about 1,000 km (700 miles) north of Beijing, China's capital. It was on the former Chinese Eastern Railway (CER) in what was then known as northern Manchuria and, until China's Communist Party set up the People's Republic in 1949, was part of Heilungkiang Province. A Mongol trading town, in 1905 it was declared a foreign treaty-port town. When part of Japan's puppet-state of Manchukuo (1932–45), it was called Lupin.

● BELOW
A Class VL80S electric-locomotive stands on shed awaiting its turn of duty.

● BELOW
This 2-10-0 Ty4 109 former Deutsche Reichsbahn Class 44 was a German Army engine in World War II and formerly S160 Tr203 229 of the United States Army Transport Corps (USATC). It is pictured at Malbork, Poland, in 1974. The city, a railway junction, was assigned to Poland in 1945. Formerly part of East Prussia, it had been known as Marienburg.

varying forms, making them the most numerous steam-class in world history.

The express-passenger streamline P36 Class 4-8-4 was the last main-line express-type built in the USSR, the first example appearing in 1950. This was a successful locomotive with many modern features and graceful lines. About 250 were built by Kolomna Locomotive Works, between 1954-56.

The S Class 2-6-2 standard express-locomotives, of which more than 4,000 were built, is the most numerous passenger-class in the world. It was introduced in 1910, and building continued until 1951.

● PARTY CONGRESS PHASES OUT SYSTEM

In February 1956 the Communist Party Congress declared that steam should be phased out. That year, all steam construction ceased.

Today, nearly a fifth of the standard gauge has been electrified. The basic freight-hauler on a.c. lines is the eight-twin-unit type VL80. The d.c. system uses VL10 Bo-Bo twin units – also made in a four-unit version.

Passenger electrics are supplied by the Skoda company from its works in the Czech Republic. The most numerous is the CS4T Bo–Bo for a.c. lines.

Diesel-powered freights are hauled by TE3 and 21762 12-axle twin-unit locomotives. To cope with ever-longer trains, three-and four-unit sets have been built – the 3TEIOM, 4TEIOS and 4TE130S Series.

Diesel passenger trains use the Skoda-made TEP60 in one- or twin-unit sets. A TEP70 series of Co-Cos developing 4,000 hp per unit and weighing 129 tonnes has been introduced for longer, 25- to 30-car passenger-trains. These units have a maximum speed of more than 178 kph (110 mph).

THE MIDDLE EAST

The former Hejaz Pilgrim Route to Mecca forms an important part of the railway networks of Syria and Jordan. The route, built to the 3 ft 5¼ in gauge, still sees steam operation in both countries. Syria also has a standard-gauge network, which originated with the Baghdad Railway. This passed through Aleppo, north-west Syria. The former Prussian G8 0-8-0s and British War Department 2-10-0s used on these lines all disappeared in 1976. The system has been diesel-operated ever since.

Jordan Railways operates between Der'a in Syria on the border with Jordan, southwards towards Saudi Arabia. The Pilgrim Route originally went as far south as Medina, but the northern reaches in Saudi Arabia have long since been abandoned. Mecca, the ultimate destination, was never reached. In 1975, Jordan Railways opened a branch to Aqaba on the Gulf of Arabia extension of the Red Sea. Jordan's last steam locomotives were a batch of Japanese Pacifics. Its steam survives as Mikado 2-8-2s.

IRAQI STATE RAILWAYS METRE-GAUGE Z CLASS 2-8-2	
Date	1955–6
Builder	Esslingen, Baden-Württemberg, West Germany
Client	Iraqi State Railways
Gauge	Metre
Driving wheels	4 ft
Capacity	Cylinders 18 x 24 in
Total weight	68 tons

● **ABOVE**
One of the Moguls built by Borsig of Berlin in 1911 for the Baghdad Railway rolls on to the pier at Hisarönü on the Black Sea coast of Turkey in Asia.

● **OPPOSITE ABOVE LEFT**
A scene on Syria's Hejaz Railway between Damascus and Der'a in Syria, on the border with Jordan. The engine is No. 91, a Hartmann 2-8-0 built to the Hejaz 1.05 metre gauge.

● **BELOW LEFT**
A quartet of modern diesels standing outside Haifa depot, Israel.

● **BELOW RIGHT**
A 2-8-0 engine built by Borsig of Berlin in 1914, pictured at Der'a from which it worked the twice-weekly mixed-traffic train branch to Busra in southern Syria.

● **JORDANIAN PHOSPHATES**

Another railway organization in Jordan is the Aqaba Railway Corporation (ARC). This began operations in 1979, to carry phosphates from mines at Al Hassa and later from Wadi el Abyad to Aqaba. General Electric 100-ton 2,000-hp Co-Co diesel-electrics are used and are powerful units for the Middle Eastern gauge.

Abdul Aziz ibn Saud (1880–1953), the first King of Saudi Arabia (1932–53), was keen on railways. He promoted a standard-gauge line about 600 km (370 miles) long to connect Ryadh – the joint capital with Mecca – with Ad Dammām,

the town on the Gulf opposite Bahrain, and the related oilfield at Damman. Diesel-electric Bo-Bos and Co-Cos were used from the outset. In the 1970s, a consortium worked on plans to re-open the Jejaz southwards from Jordan. Many field-surveys were made, but work did not proceed.

● **ACCESS TO MEDITERRANEAN SEA**

Iraq's railways comprise a mixture of metre- and standard-gauge systems. Iraq has an outstandingly keen will to develop its railways, by modernizing and by building new lines. One such is

westwards from Baghdad through Syria, to provide access to the Mediterranean Sea. Investment in powerful diesel-locomotives has been made for standard-gauge lines, using 3,600 hp engines. Iraqi Railways has about 450 diesel-electrics in service, mainly on standard gauge. It retains 75 steam locomotives on its books for metre-gauge use in the south.

Iran phased out steam in the 1950s in favour of General Motors (GM) diesel-electrics.

Israel's 900 km (560 mile) railway system is also fully diesel-operated.

● **ABOVE RIGHT**
A Jordanian Railways Hejaz 2-8-2 engine built by Jung in 1955 at the shed in Amman, the Jordanian capital, in 1979.

● **RIGHT**
A brace of Syrian 1.05 metre-gauge 2-6-0 tanks built by SLM of Switzerland in 1894 raise steam at Sergayah on the Syrian-Lebanese border before returning to Damascus, the Syrian capital, with excursion-trains.

INDIAN STEAM TRAINS

India's final steam-development phase was irretrievably influenced by American designs, which flooded into the country in World War II. The American engines' simple, robust construction, free steaming and accessibility to moving parts suited Indian conditions. When new standard designs were required for the broad gauge, to replace the ageing British X Series, India turned to American practice.

● **WP EXPRESS-PASSENGER ENGINE**
After talks with Baldwin in the mid-1940s and before independence in 1947, the WP express-passenger engine was conceived specifically for Indian conditions. The first batch was delivered in 1947. They proved successful, well-balanced, free steaming and – because of their 18-ton axleload – capable of rolling heavy trains at 60 mph. Building continued over a 20-year period and the class totalled 755 engines.

CLASS WT 2-8-4T	
Date	1959
Builder	Chittaranjan Locomotive Works, Chittaranjan, West Bengal
Client	Indian Railways
Gauge	5 ft 6 in
Driving wheels	Diameter 5 ft 7 in
Capacity	Cylinders 20 x 28 in
Total weight in full working order	123 tons

A heavyfreight version was introduced in 1950, classified WG. These had the same boiler, motion and other parts standard with the WP but smaller driving wheels and larger cylinders. Again, they were a complete success, and the class had reached 2,450 examples when building ended in 1970.

As the years passed, WGs often worked turnabout with WPs on express-passenger duties for increasing numbers of diesel engines, and electric engines were used on India's heaviest freight-trains. It is a tribute to the American engines' design that there was little tangible difference between them.

The suitability of American engines after World War II resulted from changing conditions in India. Maintenance, track condition and general standards of workmanship not being

● **LEFT**
Indian Railways operated 30 of these massive 2-8-4 tanks, designed in India for heavy suburban services. Their coupled wheels and cylinders were the same dimensions as the WP Pacifics, but the boiler was smaller. This example, taking water at Rajahmundry, did cross-country traffic work around the Godavari Delta, Andhra Pradesh State.

● OPPOSITE
WPs were standard express-passenger power across India over the last 30 years of steam but no two were ever exactly alike. Many had delightful ornamentation and decoration.

what they once were. A lighter Pacific was needed for the more restricted routes in the North West and 104 examples of the WL Class went into service. These engines, built in 1955–68, have a 17-ton axleload.

● END OF STEAM

A similar locomotive standardization applied on India's huge network of metre-gauge lines with the introduction of the YP Pacific and related YG 2-8-2 in the early 1950s. The metre-gauge YL 2-6-2s – with an axleload of eight tons – appeared in 1952 to complete a trio of standard designs.

As dieselization and electrification advanced, India, popularly regarded as the world's last great steam country, began to lose its steam heritage. Steam ended on the broad-gauge main lines in 1995. By the end of 1996, the metre gauge was but a shadow of its former self. On the erstwhile narrow gauge, diesels and closures had taken their toll, almost decimating a fascinating, extremely diversified group of veterans.

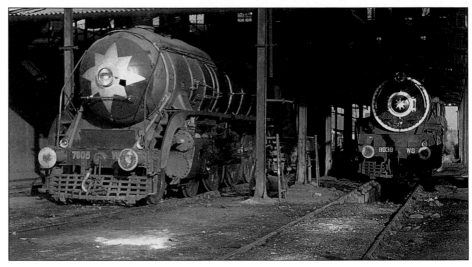

● TOP

Each year, Indian Railways held a locomotive beauty competition. Each regional railway was invited to submit an ornately embellished WP for the grand judging in Delhi, India's capital. Here, engine No. 7247, the Eastern Railway's exhibit, leaves the depot at Asansol, West Bengal, before proceeding to Delhi.

● ABOVE

This depot scene on the 5 ft 6 in gauge lines shows a WP Pacific (left) and a WG Class 2-8-2 (right). These post-World War II Indian Standards totalled more than 3,000 locomotives.

● LEFT

Northern India's sugar-plantation lines have many vintage locomotives running on 2 ft gauge systems. Most locomotives are of British or Continental European origin, augmented by a batch of Baldwin 4-6-0s built for military service in Europe in World War I and pensioned off to India for further use. A veteran takes water on the Katauli system.

INDIA GOES ELECTRIC

India's first electric-trains were operating before the famous X Series standard steam locomotives entered service in the late 1920s. By the 1930s, extensive electrification was operating over the two main lines from Bombay on the Great Indian Peninsular Railway (GIPR). This was encouraged by the long climb to the Deccan Plateau through the Ghats. Two routes, one to Calcutta, one to Madras, involved a 600 m

● LEFT
An Indian Government Railways WAM4 Co-Co freight-train.

INDIAN RAILWAYS (IR) ELECTRIC LOCOMOTIVE CLASS WAM4	
Date	1971
Builders	Chittaranjan Locomotive Works, Chittaranjan, Damodar Valley, West Bengal OR Bihar State, India
Client	Indian Railways
Gauge	5 ft 6 in
Line voltage	25 k V a.c.
Wheel arrangement	Co-Co
Weight	113 tons

(2,000 ft) climb on 2.5 per cent grades. The locomotives were from Metropolitan Vickers 2-Co-1s for passenger operation and a C-C with coupling-rod drive for freight. Operations were on 1.5kV d.c.

● **THE DISAPPEARANCE OF STEAM**

India had a long transition period from steam to diesel and electric. It was to be another 65 years before main-line steam disappeared. One of the 4-6-0 passenger designs from the BESA Series early in the century was still being built in 1951.

By the mid-1950s the aim of Indian Railways was to advance electrification and diesel as a general policy. Electrification was the preferred mode, the country having an abundance of coal and, at that time, no indigenous oil industry. Electrification of main long-distance lines was sound investment in a country with so vast a population and a railway system that was

the lifeline of a surging economy. By 1961, 718 km (446 miles) of broad-gauge line were electrified. This rose to 3,540 km (2,200 miles) over the following decade.

Electrification of suburban services in Calcutta, both Howrah and Sealdah, used the 25 kV a.c. system, which was to become an Indian standard. The standard diesel-electric locomotive WDM1 from America was followed by many standard WDM4s, which were Alco-designed and built at the diesel-locomotive works at Varanasi, Uttar Pradesh State. Later, electric-locomotives adopted many features of these six-motor workhorses.

● **INDIAN-BUILT ELECTRIC-LOCOMOTIVES**

In 1962 the first Indian-built electric-locomotive appeared from Chittaranjan Locomotive Works near Asansol in West Bengal. The WCM-type, 3,600 hp engine

● RIGHT
In June 1994, Air Foyle/Antonov transported the world's first "flying" train – a 109 tonne diesel locomotive from Canada to Ireland.

● **RIGHT**
A brand-new Class WAG 6C Co-Co 25 kV a.c., resplendent in blue-and-white livery.

● **BELOW LEFT**
One of 1,200 electric multiple units owned by India's Northern Railway pictured on the line between New Delhi and Palwal, a place of great antiquity important to Aryan traditions, in Haryana State, south-east of Delhi.

● **BELOW RIGHT**
A Class WAP 1-25 passenger Co-Co of India's Northern Railway about to depart.

was for the Central Railways d.c. line. In 1964, India's first a.c. electric-locomotive was the WHE1 Bo-Bo, designed by a European consortium.

By the 1970s, Indian Railways operated 600 electric-locomotives and more than 1,100 diesels, 700 of which were standard WDM2 2,500 hp Co-Cos. A year later, Chittaranjan built its last steam locomotive, a YG Class 2-8-2 for the metre gauge. India's first key route to be electrified was the main line between Delhi and Calcutta. Next came Delhi-Madras, Delhi-Bombay, Calcutta-Madras-Bombay. By 1987, about 8,000 km (5,000 miles) had been electrified.

● **SELF-SUFFICIENCY**
The days when India imported vast packages of locomotives and rolling stock, mainly from Britain, are

history. The country is self-sufficient in all aspects of railway production, with hi-tech plants and skilled production. The locomotive industry developed in India since the 1960s has enabled steam to be phased out on the

broad gauge. Metre-gauge systems with YP and YG Pacifics and Mikados remaining in certain areas, especially the Western and North-East Frontier Railways, were expected to be phased out in 1997.

● **LEFT**
This locomotive built by Alco waits for the right of way.

CHINESE LOCOMOTIVES

The Steam Age has been in decline across the world since the 1950s. By 1970 steam had disappeared from large areas, notably North America, Britain and most of Europe. In the mid-1970s, the fact that China was still building steam-locomotives at the rate of more than one a day was worldwide news reported extensively by the media.

● DATONG AND TANGSHAN

China's main building centre was at Datong, west of Beijing, in Shanxi Province, close to the border with the Inner Mongolian Autonomous Region. The area is noted for hot summers and bitterly cold winters when temperatures drop to minus-20 degrees Celsius.

Datong, opened in 1959, built steam-engines based on a 1950s design from the Soviet Union. It produced two standard classes: the Qianjin (Forward) Class, QJ 2-10-2, freight, first produced in 1965, and the JS 2-8-2 for general purposes. Some of these engines were

being sent to new lines as railway building continued apace in China.

Shortly after activity at Datong was discovered by the West, news came of another works, producing locomotives for industrial use. It was located in Tangshan, a coalmining and industrial centre about 260 km (160 miles) east of Beijing, in Hebei Province. Tangshan had produced the Shangyang (Aiming at the Sun) or SY Class locomotive, but had been largely destroyed by an earthquake

in 1976. The quake was unparalleled in modern history, with a 242,000 death-toll from a population of 1.06 million. The city was rapidly rebuilt and steam-locomotive production continued. Tangshan has built about 1,700 SY Mikados.

Datong finished building steam in the late 1980s. In summer 1996, however, continued building at Tangshan was confirmed, albeit on a reduced scale.

● **ABOVE**
A QJ Class 2-10-2 locomotive is assembled in the erecting shop.

● **LEFT**
A brace of QJs resides amid the smoky gloom of the steam-testing shed at Datong works. Both locomotives have spent the day running trials on the specially constructed test-track.

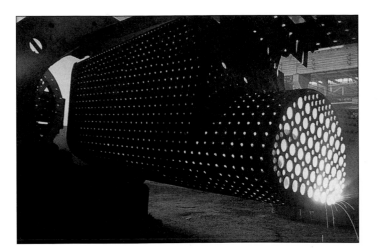

● STEAM BUILDING

Other works built steam locomotives for China's 762 mm gauge forestry lines. These are standard 28-ton 0-8-0 engines. Isolated building of these may have continued.

To witness steam-building is unforgettable. A vast shop contained 20 or more boilers in varying stages of construction. Inner and outer fireboxes contrasted with boiler shells. All was illuminated and silhouetted in ghostly patterns by the welders' blinding flashes and set to a deafening cacophony of heavy drilling. The memories flooded back – Crewe, Derby, Doncaster, Swindon it mattered not, as if by time-machine the witness was back among the living vitality of the Steam Age, and something for many years suspected was confirmed: the Steam Age was every bit as fabulous as remembered.

(Q J) C L A S S 2 - 1 0 - 2	
Date	1957
Builder	Datong & Dalian
Client	China Railways
Gauge	4 ft 8½ in
Driving wheels	1,500 mm
Capacity	2 cylinders 650 x 800 mm

● **TOP LEFT**
Welding an inner-firebox at the Datong Locomotive Works, Datong, Shanxi Province, China.

● **TOP RIGHT**
Welding-operations on cylinders and smokebox saddle for a QJ Class 2-10-2 engine.

● **ABOVE**
Measuring tolerances of machining on a QJ Class 2-10-2's driving-axle.

● **LEFT**
QJ Class 2-10-2 driving wheels in the foreground. The locomotive behind is waiting to leave the erecting shop for steaming trials.

China's Working Steam

Steam's rapid decline in India in the 1990s has left China by far the biggest user. In 1996, China had about 6,500 steam-locomotives at work. This is far more than the rest of the world put together. When India had 6,500 active locomotives, they comprised more than 150 different types. China's centralized planning has meant there have been just five types – only three main-liners, one industrial and one narrow-gauge type predominate.

● MAIN-LINERS

Of the main-liners, most are QJ class 2-10-2s of which about 3,000 are active. These are followed by the JS Class 2-8-2 with about 1,300 examples, backed up by a mere 25 survivors of the once-numerous JF Class 2-8-2. The SY Class 2-8-2 industrial accounts for another 1,700 engines. On 762 mm gauge lines about 500 standard 0-8-0s bring the total to some 6,500 locomotives. In contrast with the ubiquitous QJs are the JF Mikados, now rapidly disappearing from main-line service. These were the forerunners of the JS Class and once numbered more than 2,000 locomotives. The earliest ones date back to 1918.

Most of China's rail-connected heavy industries use SY Class 2-8-2s. Many are

● BELOW
An industrial SY Class 2-8-2, built at Tangshan, tips molten slag down the slag bank at Anshan Iron and Steel Works. Anshan, in Liaoning Province, is China's steel capital.

● LEFT
The daily workmen's passenger-train heads across the 700 mm gauge rails of the Anxiang in north-eastern China.

● OPPOSITE
A trio of QJ Class 2-10-2s bask amid the sooty magic of the steam-locomotive sheds at Shenyang, Liaoning Province, north-eastern China.

SY CLASS INDUSTRIAL 2-8-2 (PICTURE NUMBER 2)	
Date	1969
Builder	Tangshan Locomotive Works, Hebei Province, China
Client	Industrial users across China
Gauge	Standard
Driving wheels	1,370 mm
Capacity	2 cylinders 530 x 710 mm
Total weight in full working order	143 tons

relatively new engines but are, in essence, typical light-American Mikados, the type of engine common on many American roads before World War I.

The odd main-line rarity does occur in industrial locations. In November 1996, it was confirmed that at least one KD6 Class 2-8-0 remained active. This engine is one of the famous United States Army Transportation Corps (USATC) S160s, more than 2,000 of which were built in America to the British loading gauge for World War II operations around the world.

● **UNIQUE 2,000-TON TRAINS**

China is also the only country in which steam locomotives can be seen out on main lines heading 2,000-ton trains. The mighty QJ Class often run in pairs and are put through their paces over the steep gradients presented on many main lines.

● **QJS WORKING NEW LINES**

The concept of China as a steam paradise was heightened on 1 December 1995 when a new 950 km (590 mile) long railway opened across the Inner Mongolian Autonomous Region. It is completely QJ-worked, has six

locomotive-sheds and is semaphore-signalled over much of its distance. The line runs between Tongliao, a town in the region's far east, and Jining, east of the region's capital Hohhot. The Jingpeng Pass sees double-headed QJs working up a 50 km (31 mile) bank through six tunnels, around horse-shoe curves and over a 90-degree curved viaduct.

● **ABOVE LEFT**
The pride of the Harbin shed was Zhoude, the QJ Class locomotive named in honour of Chinese Communist revolutionary hero Marshal Zhu De (1886–1976) who became Commander-in-Chief of the People's Liberation Army (PLA) and second in the Communist Party's hierarchy only to Mao Tse-tung. Zhoude is commemorated on the smokebox-doors' brass bust.

● **ABOVE RIGHT**
An industrial SY Class 2-8-2 resides in silhouette among the smoky gloom of the engine-shed at Anshan Iron and Steel Works.

MODERN CHINA

Since the establishment of the People's Republic of China in 1949, China's national system has more than doubled its track route mileage and increased its passenger and freight traffic by ten and 20 times respectively.

● CONTINUED GROWTH

From 2001 to the end of 2005 more was spent on railways and other fixed assets than in the previous 50 years. This level of investment is due to continue with the development of high-speed links. Steam will remain for some years: coal is cheap and plentiful, whereas oil is not, and the annual intake of new electric- and diesel-powered locomotives is insufficient to keep up with the expanding traffic, so that steam is being replaced only slowly.

Both standard- and narrow-gauge steam locomotives are still being made although in small numbers. By the 1980s, Chinese railway building had reached unprecedented levels. Getting at the coal had become China's most pressing transport need. Shanxi Province has a third of China's coal reserves and

● LEFT
Mainland China has only three cities with tramway systems – Changchun, Anshan and Dalian. This scene at the run-down depot in Changchun shows the decline that has set in and caused many parts of this once prolific network to be abandoned.

millions of tons were lying on the ground awaiting conveyance. At present, coal accounts for well over 50 per cent of freight on China's four major rail trunk lines. These are:

- Beijing – Guangzhou.
- Shenyang – Lanzhou – Lianun Gang.
- Beijing – Shanghai.
- Harbin – Dalian.

Lanzhou (Lanchow) is in Gansu (Kansu) Province. Llanyun Gang (Lienyun Harbour) is in Jiangsu (Kiangsu) Province. Harbin is in Heilongjiang (Heilungkiang) Province. Dalian (Talian) is in Liaoning Province.

Many diesels have been built since the late 1950s and by the 1980s 20 per cent of China's railway traffic was diesel-

● ABOVE LEFT
In Liaoning Province, the shape of things to come on the main line between Shenyang and Dalian, which until the late 1980s was one of China's most famous steam-operated main lines. A freight-train heads away from Shenyang and passes beneath the Fushun line at the Hunhe River. Fushun, north-east of Shenyang, works China's largest opencast coalmine.

● LEFT
A China Railways Co-Co diesel hydraulic locomotive, Class DFH3, heads a passenger-train between the cities of Jilin and Changchun, in Jilin Province, north-eastern China. Changchun was developed by the Japanese as capital of their puppet-state of Manchukuo (1932–45).

● **RIGHT**
A brace of China Railway's DF4 class diesel-electric locomotives head a freight-train past Zoujia on the Changchun to Jilin line in January 1994.

CHINESE RAILWAYS CLASS DF4 DIESEL ELECTRIC

Date	1969
Builder	Dalian Locomotive Works, Liaoning Province, China
Client	Chinese Railways
Gauge	4 ft 8½ in
Wheel arrangement	Co-Co
Weight	138 tonnes
Maximum speed	100 kph

hauled. A large fleet of locally built 3300 Dong Feng (East Wind) 4 freight Co-Cos is expected to reach more than 4,000 units by the end of the century. In the early 1980s, General Electric (GE) supplied more than 200 Type C36-7 4,000 hp Co-Co diesel electrics for freight-haulage. A repeat order for 200 locomotives three years later was placed with the same company.

● **DEMAND EXCEEDS SUPPLY**

A 5,000 hp Dong Feng Co-Co is the standard passenger diesel locomotive. Expansion of diesel and electric traction is inadequate to keep up with demand, so Class QJ 2-10-2s and Class JS 2-8-2 continue to be used.

Priority in the early 1990s was to electrify the double-track coal-line from the railhead in Shanxi Province to the port of Qinhuangdao, Hebei Province, as well as the 322 km (200 mile) coal route from Datong, Inner Mongolia, south to Taiyuan, capital of Shanxi Province.

The building of new lines and further electrification is to increase the coal-carrying capacity, because China's domestic needs are 70 per cent met by coal. Coal is also a top foreign revenue-earner with millions of tonnes being exported yearly. To serve the newly electrified lines, Chinese builders have supplied 138-tonne Shaoshan SS3-type electric-locomotives. Demand is so great, however, that 80 microprocessor-equipped, thyristor-controlled, 138-tonne, 4,800 kV Co-Cos have been bought from Japan, as well as 100 electric-locomotives from Russia.

● **LEFT**
Harbin, the capital of Heilongjiang Province in north east China, once had a tramway network. By the late 1980s, this was down to one line. This picture was taken at Harbin tram depot in the final year of operation.

JAPANESE FREIGHT

Japanese railways were largely built to the 3 ft 6 in narrow gauge, to save money crossing often mountainous terrain. Gauge and terrain meant slow services. Then, road services started to compete. New motorways, often built along shorter, more direct routes, allowed shorter journey-times. The railways had to respond and the solution devised for the passenger service was the Shinkansen.

● EFFICIENT MOVEMENT OF LARGE TONNAGES

The solution for freight-traffic was not so positive but followed the practice in most other countries of focusing on what railborne traffic could do best, the efficient movement of large tonnages over a limited number of routes. This can be either block-loads of bulk commodities such as stone or ore, or containerized-traffic where handling-costs can be minimized. Despite this concentration on particular types of

● BELOW

JR Freight locomotives on-shed at Shin Kawasaki depot. Right, EF 66 29, a 1968-built mixed-traffic locomotive. Several locomotive classes have the same body style, being built to work under different catenary voltages. Left, EF 200 8, an early 1990s design. As the legend on the side indicates, this uses inverter technology.

● OPPOSITE
Chichibu Railway electric locomotive No. 103 on a freight-working at Chichibu, Honshu, in 1995. The freight-services run all week and are also fairly frequent on Saturdays.

traffic, freight is still loss-making. Traffic fell from 68.6 million tonnes in 1985 to 58.4 million tonnes in 1991. The number of marshalling yards has been cut, from 110 to 40 in 1986. Freight-train-kilometres were cut by 25 per cent in 1985 alone.

● BREAK-UP OF JAPANESE RAILWAYS

As part of the break-up of Japanese railways, which started in 1987, JR Freight was formed to operate all freight services. The company owns its own locomotives (1,069 in 1994), wagons and terminals, paying passenger-companies for the use of their tracks.

Only a couple of the private railway companies operate freight-trains. The Chichibu Railway, serving Chichibu, 50 km (30 miles) north-west of Tokyo, runs more freight than any other private company, linking a limestone quarry and a cement works to the JR network.

● ABOVE
JR diesel DE10 1521, a shunting and trip-working locomotive. These 1966-built diesel-hydraulic locomotives have the unusual wheel arrangement AAA-B. They work at many of the few stations that still have a freight-terminal. The engine is pictured at Fuji, Honshu, in 1994, which is below the 3,775 m (12,388 ft) high sacred mountain, Japan's highest peak, known as Fuji-no-Yama, 113 km (70 miles) south-west of Tokyo. Its volcano last erupted in 1649.

● BELOW
Electric locomotive EF 65 22 on a container-train at Odawara on the original Tokaido line, in 1994. This locomotive class was introduced in 1964. It shares body design with other classes, as well as with exported designs, notably locomotives built under licence in Spain. Odawara is a town in Kanagawa Prefecture, south-eastern Honshu, the largest of Japan's four chief islands and considered as Japan's mainland. Odawara is 80 km (50 miles) south-west of Tokyo (ancient Edo or Yedo). Tokaido is the great coastal road along the Pacific Ocean between Tokyo and Kyoto, Japan's capital until 1869 and a great manufacturing centre, along the Kanto Plain beneath the Kanto Mountains. Tokaido means "Eastern Sea Route".

CLASS EF 66 ELECTRIC LOCOMOTIVE

Year into service	1968
Builders	Mechanical: Kawasaki Heavy Industries, Japan Electrical: Tokyo Shibaura Electric Co., Tokyo, Japan
Gauge	1,067 mm
Catenary voltage	1,500 kV d.c.
Wheel arrangement	B-B-B
Rated output	3,900 kW
Weight in working order	100 tonnes
Maximum service speed	120 kph

Japan's "Bullet Train"

Japan's "Bullet Train", called Shinkansen – Japanese for New Super Express – was developed to provide fast, regular and reliable passenger-services between main conurbations.

All the routes were to be newly built and segregated from the rest of the network. This allowed them to be constructed to standard gauge rather than to the narrow 3 ft 6 in (1,067 mm) gauge of the national railway system. The lines were to be designed for high speed, the initial expectation being to operate eventually at 250 kph.

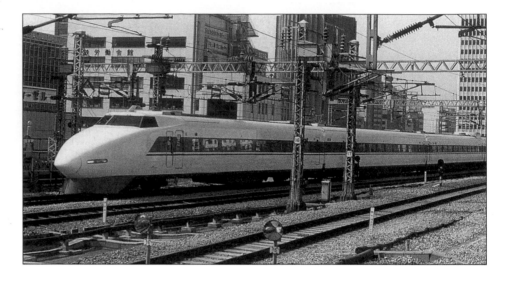

● **ABOVE**
A 100-Series Shinkansen arriving at Tokyo Station in 1994.

● **TOKAIDO LINE**

The first route, the Tokaido line on Honshu, opened in 1964 in time for the Olympic Games that year. It ran between Tokyo and, about 400 km (250 miles) away, Osaka, Japan's second city in size and the industrial metropolis of the Orient, via Nagoya and Kyoto. Three further routes subsequently opened on Honshu:

● The Sanyo line running south across the country from Osaka.

● **BELOW**
An E-2 Series "Max" Shinkansen E153 102 at Utsunomiya, Honshu, in 1994. These double-deck super expresses were built to increase capacity on commuter and holiday services on lines north of Tokyo.

● The Joetsu line crossing the country from Tokyo to Niigata to the north.

● The Tohoku line running north from Tokyo to Morioka.

A branch has been built off the Tohoku line, to Yamagata, a silk-industry centre. However, this route is an upgrading and regauging of an existing line, not the full high-speed line of the other routes.

● **FIVE SERIES OF TRAINS**

The Shinkansen has five series of trains. The 0-Series are the original sets, which now run the stopping-services on the Tokaido and Sanyo lines. The 100-Series run the semi-fasts and the 300-Series the fast – Nozomi – trains, both on the Tokaido/Sanyo lines. The 200-Series run the Joetsu and Tohoku services and are distinguished by a green rather than a blue stripe along their sides. The 400-Series are short, narrow sets, which look distinctly different from the others and run the Yamagata service. The E-2 Series are double-deck sets for use on the Joetsu and Tohoku routes and have been christened "Max".

The Shinkansen are fitted with an in-cab signalling system. This can be

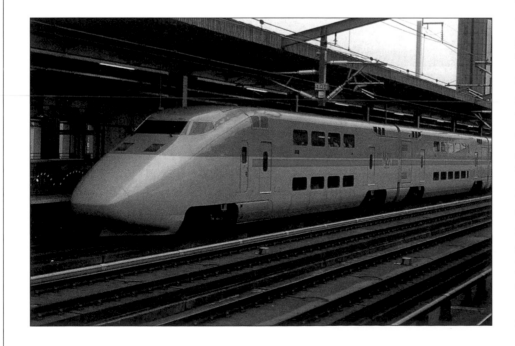

SHINKANSEN 0-SERIES TRAIN

Date	1964
Builders	Mechanical: Niigata Tekko; Hitachi Mfg Co; Kawasaki Heavy Industries, Japan Electrical: Hitachi Mfg. Co.; Tokyo Shibaura Electric Co., Mitsubishi Electric Co., Japan
Gauge	1,435 mm
Catenary voltage	a.c. 25 kV, 60 Hz
Powered axles per unit	All axles driven
Rated output per unit	11,840 kW
Maximum service speed	220 kph

seen in a driving-simulator unit at Tokyo Transport Museum. The original lines operated at 220 kph, increased to 240 kph on the northern routes. Nozomi trains run at 270 kph. It is planned to run the next generation of stock at an increased speed of 320 kph, experimental sets having run much faster.

There is a dense service pattern. For example, ten trains leave Tokyo on the Tokaido line between 08.00-09.00 hrs, six terminating at Osaka, one continuing to Okayama seaport, two to Hiroshima and one service going through to Hakata. The fastest service covers the 515 km (320 miles) to Osaka in 2 hours 32 minutes, with two intermediate stops, and overtakes four trains en route.

● **ABOVE**
A 200-Series Shinkansen 222-18 at Utsunomiya, 97 km (60 miles) north of Tokyo, in 1994. The gentleman in white is a train crew-member. This station is the terminus of the JR branch line to Nikko, one of Japan's main centres for temples and shrines, a city and mountain resort at 609 m (2,000 ft) in the Nikko Mountains of central Honshu Island.

● **BELOW**
A 0-Series Shinkansen at Shin Fuji in 1994, one of many stations, which allow fast trains to overtake the stopping-services. The much-photographed section of route, with Mount Fuji as a backdrop, is just north of this station.

JAPANESE MULTIPLE UNITS

Japanese Railways (JR) have a long history of electrification. By 1991, 11,700 km (7,300 miles), 58 per cent of the total JR network, were electrified. Intensive operation of many lines has led to significant use of multiple unit trains. Although only 58 per cent of the lines are electrified, electric multiple units (EMUs) outnumbered diesel multiple units (DMUs) by a far greater proportion. In 1991, there were 3,189 diesel-powered passenger-coaches (13 per cent) and 20,548 electric-coaches (87 per cent).

Multiple Units exist in each segment of Japan's railways – both private and JR, suburban, outer-suburban and long-distance (and high-speed if Shinkansen are included), as well as in the luxury-train market. The EMU's variants and history are vast.

● LEFT
JR suburban EMU No. 22-23 at Akihabara, Tokyo, in 1994. This is a variation on the standard design suburban EMU. On suburban networks, each line's trains are painted a different colour, the same colour as used on network diagrams. The crowd waits on a Saturday morning when the service operates every ten minutes.

The two most common EMU designs, of which there are many variants, are the suburban set and the outer-suburban set. The Odakyu EMU represents the many small builds of specialist EMUs. The Class 165 EMU described in the technical box represents about 20 classes of trains built during 1959–71 for the railway's different electrical systems and with small changes in detail. This example runs in three-coach sets. Other variants run in sets of up to ten coaches.

● DISTINCTIVE DESIGNS

Private railways run a variety of EMUs. Some have a JR pedigree, either secondhand or to similar designs. Many railway companies, however, have developed their own often distinctive designs.

Because electrification focused on busier routes, most lines around the main conurbations are operated by electric traction. DMUs, being limited to through-services from lesser-used routes, are seldom seen in such built-up areas. Diesel-powered services tend to increase the farther you travel from Tokyo. They are concentrated on the northern and south-western ends of the main island, Honshu, and on the two islands of Hokkaido and Kyushu, respectively Japan's second- and third-largest islands.

● RIGHT
Shonan monorail EMU 505 approaching Ofuna, south of Yokohama, Honshu, in 1994. This line, built in 1970, connects JR's Tokaido line with Enoshima resort area. It has steep gradients and two tunnels. It is a means of transport, not a tourist or showground operation.

JAPANESE RAILWAY (JR) CLASS 165 ELECTRIC MULTIPLE UNIT (EMU)

Date	1962
Builders	Mechanical: Nippon Sharyo Seizo Ltd, Kinki Nihon Sharyo and Hitachi Mfg Co., Japan Electrical: Hitachi Mfg Co., Mitsubishi Electric Co., Tokyo Shibaura Electric Co., Japan
Gauge	1,067 mm
Catenary voltage	d.c. 1,500 kV
Configuration	Two power-cars per three-car unit
Wheel arrangement	Four powered axles per power-car
Rated output	480 kW per power-car
Weight in working order	108 tonnes per three-car set
Maximum service speed	110 kph

● THE KASHIMA COASTAL RAILWAY ON HONSHU

All train categories exist as DMUs, ranging from two-axle railbuses, through rural all-station stopping-trains, to luxury-express units. Vehicle design has tended to follow that of EMUs, with small modifications to allow for engines.

Many of Japan's private railway companies are commuter operations which were electrified many years ago and operate large fleets of EMUs. However, some of these companies also operate DMUs, not only for rural stopping-train services but for other services as well. An example is the Kashima Coastal Railway (KRT) on Honshu. It runs DMUs on an 80 km route east of Tokyo, built in 1985, using both a high-capacity design and a streamlined version for its express services.

● **ABOVE**
An express-EMU of Odakyu Railway (OER) approaching Shinjuku Station, inner Tokyo, in 1994. The OER, like many private railways, has several express EMUs, in addition to its large fleet of suburban trains. It serves a resort area south-west of Tokyo. Shinjuku Station is the world's busiest station, being served by JR, two private railways and several underground lines.

● **ABOVE**
JR outer-suburban EMU No. 401-76 at Ishioka, 64 km (40 miles) north-east of Tokyo, in 1995. This is representative of a widely used design, the 1960 multivoltage (1,500 volt d.c. and 20 kV, 50 Hz) version of the Class 165. The livery represents a group of routes, similarly to suburban trains. Background: DMUs of the Kashima Railway, Honshu.

● **BELOW**
Electric-railcars Nos. 109 and 108 of the Hakone Tozan Railway near Gora, Honshu. This 15 km (9 mile) line climbs 450m (1,477 ft) by means of three dead-end reverses and up gradients of up to 8 per cent. These trains, from 1927, were operating in 1994. Hakone is a mountain resort with hot springs and wonderful views of Mount Fuji, 32 km (20 miles) to the north-east.

JAPANESE LONG-DISTANCE PASSENGER SERVICES

Japan's narrow-gauge railways and often mountainous terrain have prevented its railways competing successfully with the increasing competition of motorways and airways. The main response for passenger-services was the Shinkansen. However, long-distance passenger services still exist, although far fewer than 40 years ago. This is often the result of the opening of high-speed lines, which cause inter-city services to be remodelled to feed into the Shinkansen. Where new lines are unlikely, there are moves to increase speeds from the usual 120-kph maximum to 160 kph.

Long-distance services are in two categories: the usually EMU-operated day services and the locomotive-hauled overnight services.

The day services tend to be of limited frequency. They require compulsory seat-reservations and payment of a supplementary fare. A variety of EMUs, and some DMUs, are used on these services. Some feature passive tilt, to take

● **LEFT**
JR Blue Train sleeping-cars passing Yarakucho, Tokyo, in 1994. The streamlined body style was very modern when these were introduced.

● **LEFT**
JR EMU No. 189 508 passing Oji, near Tokyo, in 1994.

● **BELOW LEFT**
Japan Railways (JR) electric-locomotive EF 66 44 passing Yarakucho, Tokyo, towards the end of its overnight haul of a Blue Train in 1994. Note the headboard with the train's name.

curves faster. Double-deck stock, with its extra carrying capacity, features increasingly in new designs.

● **BLUE TRAINS**

The overnight trains, usually "Limited Expresses", are largely operated by a fleet of Blue Trains. These consist of coaching stock, predominantly sleepers, introduced since 1958. The sleeping-cars come in several forms. The difference between A- and B-sleepers is the bunk width. Some trains include dining-cars. Only a few include the addition of seated accommodation. These trains can be hauled by any locomotive. Those painted red with a shooting star on the side are reserved for sleeper services. "Ordinary Express" overnight trains, sometimes

● **RIGHT**
JR EMU No. 185 107 passing Hamametsucho, Tokyo, in 1994. Note the train's name display.

JAPAN RAILWAYS (JR) CLASS 185 ELECTRICAL MULTIPLE UNIT (EMU)

Date	1980
Builders	Mechanical: Niigata Tekko, Kawasaki Heavy Industries, Japan Electrical: Hitachi Mfg Co., Tokyo Shibaura Electric Co., Mitsubishi Electric Co., Japan
Gauge	1,067 mm
Catenary voltage	1,500 volt d.c.
Cars per unit	Four
Powered axles per unit	Eight
Rated output per unit	960 kW
Maximum service speed	110 kph

● **LEFT**
An accompanied car-carrying train of JR being loaded at Hamametsucho, Tokyo, in 1994. Note the unusual side-loading method. Car-drivers join the train at the same location.

with sleeping accommodation, are an endangered species.

Certain overnight trains also include wagons for accompanied cars. These are unusual for their method of loading – sideways on a pallet by fork-lift truck.

Private railways operate express stock, often with compulsory seat-reservations and supplements, but distances involved do not compare with JR's services.

● **RIGHT**
On Honshu Island, JR EMU No. 250-04 operating near Kogetsuenmae, between the Tokyo manufacturing suburb of Kawasaki and Japan's chief port, Yokohama, in 1994. These trains include seats from which passengers can see forward above the driver. This EMU is on the Tokaido line where it runs parallel with the Keihin railway, providing a fine train-watching location.

JAPANESE LIGHT RAIL AND METRO

Japan is a paradise for students of electric mass transit. It is well serviced with light railways and metros to carry its vast population from place to place. More than 100 tramways, metros and interurbans exist, most linked with one of the extensive privately owned electrified railway networks. Definition is difficult, because interurbans can run down the street like tramways; metros can carry interurban trains; and railways, which started off as interurbans, today provide a dense network of express, limited-stop and stopping-trains to carry people into Japan's crowded towns and cities. In terms of transit interest, some say Japan has everything Switzerland can offer and more. With most of the 120 million population crammed into

● **BELOW**
Kochi, on Shikoku, Japan's fourth-largest island, is a seaport city but the outer end of its tramway displays a rural village aspect. It is single-track with passing loops. The Hitachi Co. built Tram 201 in 1950.

25 per cent of the land area, efficient rail transit is of the utmost importance. The biggest cities have underground or elevated metro systems.

● **METROS AND TRAMWAYS**

Tokyo's extensive metro has been developed partly with private capital. The result is two separate networks, three different gauges, with overhead and third-rail current-collection. Patronage is heavy, with ten-car trains and, at peak periods, pushers employed at some points to ensure train-doors close on the crush of passengers. In addition, some private railways running into Tokyo operate underground in the city. Through-operation of private railways on to urban metros can be found in Kobe and Osaka on Honshu and with JR trains at Fukuoka, the seaport on Hakata Bay, Kyushu Island. Sapporo's Metro on Hokkaido Island features rubber-tyred trains and elevated tracks, which are covered over as protection from heavy winter snow. Sapporo was laid out in 1869 by the Japanese government as a colonizing centre for Hokkaido Island and replaced Hakodate as the island's capital.

● **BELOW**
Car 7513 is pictured on the Arakawa tramway of Tokyo Metropolitan Transport Bureau, a 12 km (8 mile) long survivor of the citywide 1,372 mm-gauge system. All stops have high platforms. The tram was built in 1962 by Niigata Engineering.

Tramways have been in decline for some years. Those in larger cities were replaced by metros. Buses replaced trams in other places. There was little development elsewhere. Hiroshima, on Honshu, is the only city that has modernized an extensive network. The city was rebuilt after receiving the world's first atomic bomb on 6 August 1945, which ended World War II. It includes an interurban line with through-operation on to the city tramways.

However, in the 1990s there are signs of an upturn in tramway fortunes. Hakodate, the seaport city of Hokkaido Island, on the Tsurgaru Strait, and Kitakushu, across the Strait of Shimonoseki opposite Honshu, have retrenched but other systems have bought new rolling stock or rebodied older cars, segregation and traffic-management are making operation more efficient and further closures seem unlikely.

● **BELOW**
The town of Gifu in central Honshu, north-west of Nagoya, shows the interaction of trams and interurbans on street and segregated track. Articulated tram Nos. 875 and 876, which formerly worked in Sapporo, runs on the urban section of the Mino line where through-operation on to the interurban requires dual-voltage cars. Mino is 20km (12 miles) north of Gifu.

● **ABOVE**
The 1,067 mm gauge tramway of Toyohashi city, on Honshu, south-east of Nagoya, has three lines totalling 23 km (14 miles). Tram 3105 pictured approaching the railway-station terminus is secondhand from the tramways of Nagoya. It was built in 1943.

TRAMWAYS

On Honshu, Tokyo's tramway is a single, largely segregated line in the southern suburbs, the survivor of a citywide system. There is also a privately operated outer suburban tramway on a private right of way. The system at Gifu, central Honshu, is a fascinating mixture of street operation and rural interurban (at different voltages) provided by a private company. Kochi, the seaport city on

HIROSHIMA ARTICULATED-TRAM

Builder	Alna Koki/Hiroshima
Gauge	1,435 mm
Power supply	600 volt d.c.
Bogie arrangement	B-2-2-B with two 120 kW motors
Overall length	26.3 metres
Unladen weight	38.4 tons
Maximum speed	80 kph

● **BELOW**
Japan's most northerly city, Sapporo on Hokkaido Island, has kept one tram-route to feed the metro. Car 255 was built in 1958 by the local railway workshops for the 1067 mm gauge system.

Shikoku Island, has a reputation for acquiring individual, secondhand trams from European systems. These are rebuilt to run as a tourist attraction within the regular service. On Honshu, Osaka's city trams were abandoned in 1969, but a suburban tramway, subsidiary of a private railway, continued operating. Other tramways have been continuously upgraded over the years and, although still legally tramways, they can be difficult to distinguish from interurban railways. One such tramway is at Enoshima, one of Honshu's popular seaside resorts.

HOME OF THE MONORAIL

Japan is also known as the home of the monorail. These offer proper urban-transit facilities in Chiba, a prosperous commercial town on the eastern shore of Tokyo Bay, and Kitakyushu. There is also the original line between Tokyo and

● **LEFT**
Japan's most modern city-tramway serves Hiroshima, Honshu, completely rebuilt since World War II. Car 3702 is one of an increasing number of modern articulated-trams. It was built in 1987 by Alna Koki.

Haneda domestic airport, and a link between Ofuna, south-west of Yokohama, and Enoshima. More recently, several guideway systems have been built, usually featuring rubber-tyred cars and automatic train operation on elevated shuttle lines to new development. Examples on Honshu are the Portliner in Kobe, Newtram in Osaka, NTS in Hiroshima and VONA in Nagoya.

Japan, with its huge home market for electric-rail vehicles, supports many rolling-stock producers. Electrical equipment features the latest in power electronics. Among large orders for railways and metros, the producers are happy to process small but quite frequent orders from tramway undertakings. There has also been secondhand dealing within the country.

● LEFT BEHIND

Most systems operate single-bogie trams but a few articulated-cars can be found in Gifu, Hiroshima, Kagoshima, the seaport on the south of Kyushu Island, and

Kitakyushu. A sign that Japan accepts it has been left behind in tramcar development and that new ideas can come from overseas is the recent announcement by Kumamoto, a city on Kyushu Island, that it has negotiated a local-assembly package for a German design of a low-floor tram of the type developed by AEG before it became part of ADtranz.

● **LEFT**
The Hankai tramway in south Osaka, Honshu, comprises two standard-gauge lines totalling 18.7 km (12 miles). Car 169, pictured here at Ebisucho terminus, is one of many veterans from 1928 still in everyday service.

● **BELOW LEFT**
Rubber-tyred guideway systems are appearing in many Japanese cities. An example is the Astram line, built in Hiroshima in 1994.

● **BELOW RIGHT**
The tramways of Hakodate on Hokkaido Island and of Tokyo on Honshu Island have in common the 1,372 mm gauge. Hakodate has received secondhand trams from the capital, but Car 3003 is a 1995-built tram constructed by Alna Koki for use on Hakodate's two-route system.

THE PACIFIC RIM

Some of the smaller countries that surround the Pacific Ocean have relatively limited railway networks.

● REPUBLIC OF KOREA

The Korean National Railroad (KNR) of South Korea has just more than 3,000 km (1,860 miles) of track, built to standard gauge, of which more than 400 km (250 miles) had been electrified by 1987. The country's major route is between the capital Seoul and the major port of Pusan. KNR is unusual in that both freight- and passenger-traffic have been growing, although this has not been enough to ensure continued profitability. New lines and extensions continue to be built as the economy expands. Electrification is being gradually extended but most services remain diesel-hauled, except Seoul's suburban services. These are interconnected with the metro, thus requiring electric multiple units (EMUs) that can operate at both 25 kV a.c. and 1,500 v d.c.

Increasing competition from coach and air services led to acceleration of the Seoul-Pusan service, with the

● LEFT
Singapore Mass Rapid Transit Corporation (SMRT) metro sets Nos. 3126 and 3111 at Yishun in 1990. Yishun is the terminus of the north-south line.

● LEFT
Standard-gauge 800 hp, diesel-electric locomotive No. 38-150 of Vietnam Railways shunting at Luu Xa in 1989. Note the mixed-gauge track.

● BELOW
KNR express diesel multiple unit (DMU) No. 132 at Yongsan in 1995. These units, introduced in 1987, run with two power-cars and five intermediate trailers. Yongsan, a southern district of Seoul, is a good location at which to observe the railways. The suburban service goes underground between here and the main station.

introduction of 150-kph diesel-sets. Improvements are continually being made to several routes by the introduction of centralized train control (CTC), which enables more efficient and consistent control of a route, thus allowing an improved, faster service.

● MALAYSIA AND SINGAPORE

Singapore does not have its own national railway system. The sole main-line railway is a line over the Johore Strait Causeway that joins the island with Malaysia, terminating at Singapore Station, and a freight-only branch to the docks. A through-service operates from Singapore to Kuala Lumpur (KL), the Malaysian capital. A luxury-tourist service also operates from Singapore via KL to Butterworth, opposite George Town, Pinang Island, Malaysia.

Singapore has a significant mass transit network. The first section of the standard-gauge, third-rail electrified metro opened in 1987. The metro has tunnelled sections in the city centre

● **RIGHT**
Vietnam Railways metre-gauge 2-6-2T steam-
locomotive No. 131 444 at Haiphong in 1989.
French influence can be seen in the
locomotive, Chinese in the rear coach.

and elevated structures through
the suburbs.

Malaysia has a metre-gauge network
totalling more than 1,600 km
(1000 miles). Its main route runs from
Singapore via KL to Butterworth.
Electrified suburban services were
introduced in KL in December 1995.
The 18 three-coach EMUs were based
on a British design, built in Hungary
with Dutch electrical systems and fitted
out in Austria.

Passenger-loads have been rising, but
there was a steady fall in freight tonnage
in the 1980s.

KOREAN NATIONAL RAILWAYS (KNR) 8000 CLASS ELECTRIC LOCOMOTIVES

Date	1972
Builders	Mechanical: Alsthom Electrical: AEG and ACEC
Gauge	1,435 mm
Catenary voltage	25 kV, 60 Hz
Wheel arrangement	Bo-Bo-Bo
Rated outputs	5,300 hp
Weight in working order	132 tons
Maximum service speed	85 kph

● **LEFT**
An Indonesian State
Railways PJKA F10
Class engine, No.
F1012, at Blitar,
Java, in 1971.
Between 1912–20,
Java and Sumatra
took delivery of 28
of these mighty 2-
12-2Ts. This engine
was built by
Hanoang in 1914.

● **VIETNAM**
Vietnam's small railway network covers
fewer than 3,000 km (1,860 miles). It is
mainly metre gauge but does have a
couple of standard-gauge routes,
including the regauged line between
Hanoi, the capital, and Haiphong, the
port and industrial centre. The railways
were devastated by the Indo-Chinese
Wars (1940–75) and continued
investment levels are still limited. Despite
these problems, a completely new line
between Hanoi and Ha Dong was opened
in 1986.

● **RIGHT**
Korean National Railways (KNR) electric-
locomotive No. 8001 at Chongnyangnii
Station, Seoul, in 1995, just arrived with a
long-distance passenger train. The French
pedigree of these locomotives is obvious.

HONG KONG SYSTEMS

The territory of Hong Kong boasts three tramways, two on Hong Kong Island and one in the New Territories (NT). On the island, the funicular-railway Peak Tram between Garden Road and Victoria Gap, 397 m (1,303 ft) above sea level, with 1:2 gradients, celebrated its centenary in 1988. It has since been modernized. The north-shore tramway on the island was opened in 1904 and runs double-deck cars. The Hong Kong Tramways line, built to 1,067 mm gauge, runs for just under 17 km (11 miles) along the northern side of the island, through the Central District business, administrative and shopping areas of the capital, Victoria. All trams are two-axle cars operating off a 500 volt d.c. power

supply. They were all rebuilt in the tramway's own workshops in the past ten years and now carry new bodies on old trucks. The 163 trams comprise the only all-double-deck fleet in the world. There was a fear that the Victoria tram line would close when the parallel Mass Transit Railway (MTR) metro line was opened. However, while there was a

distinct drop in tram traffic, the tram's advantage for short journeys and as a metro-feeder has kept it in business. This is shown by the service pattern. Broadly, the tramway is a single-line of route but there are, typically, six separate routes operated between different turning-circles. Only a small proportion of trams operate over the full route.

● **ABOVE RIGHT**
A 12-coach commuter-train of the Kowloon-Canton Railway (KCR) near Fanling, NT in 1996 is externally similar to MTR units. Internally, however, it is far more comfortable, with higher seating capacity on transverse seats.

● **RIGHT**
In Hong Kong's New Territories (NT) Light-Rail Transit (LRT) Car 1022 is pictured at Yau Oi on route 720 to Tin Shui Wai in 1996. Note the 910 mm high platforms provided where there is street running.

TUEN MUN LIGHT-RAIL TRANSIT (LRT) CAR

Date	1988
Builders	Mechanical: Cars 1001–70 Comeng, Australia. Cars 1071–90 Kawaski Heavy Industrial, Japan. Cars 1201–10 Duewag, Germany (bogies) Electrical: Thyristor Control, Siemens, Propulsion, AEG, Germany
Operator	Kowloon Canton Railway Company
Gauge	1,435 mm
Catenary voltage	d.c. 750 volt
Overall length	19.4 m (63 ft 8 in)
Weight in working order	27.444 tonnes
Rating	390 kW (523 hp)
Maximum service speed	80 kph

● RIGHT
A double-headed train of cattle-vans filled with livestock pictured in 1996 heading for Kowloon, squeezed between the frequent electric multiple units (EMUs) on the Kowloom-Canton Railway (KCR).

The fleet has two special vehicles, Nos. 28 and 128, used for tourist services such as the daily Dim Sum tours. These also have new bodies, albeit designed, by the addition of brass fittings, to look old-fashioned. All service-cars carry advertising livery. It provides more than 10 per cent of the company's total revenue.

Apart from the double-deck cars tramway, there are three public rail systems in the territory.

● KOWLOON – CANTON RAILWAY

The Kowloon-Canton Railway (KCR) links the territory with Canton, the capital of Canton Province of China.

Construction of the 34 km (21 mile) long British section between Tsimshatsui at the tip of Kowloon and Lo Wu on the Sino-British border in the NT began in 1905. The line was opened on 1 October 1910. The whole 179 km (111 miles) was opened on 5 August 1911.

From 14 October 1949 to 4 April 1979 there were no through-passenger services except for infrequent, secret visits by Chinese leaders. Services terminated either side of the border. In the British sector, diesels replaced steam for all traffic, but electrification and modernization, completed on 15 July 1983, saw the introduction of electric multiply units (EMUs) for passenger work.

● MASS TRANSIT RAILWAY (MTR)

The first section of the Mass Transit Railway (MTR) linking the island and Kowloon by a submerged-tube tunnel opened in 1979. It is 15 km (9.3 miles) long and largely underground. A 10.8 km (6.7 mile) branch goes to the NT industrial town of Tsuen Wan. The units were supplied by Metro-Cammell of Britain. They operate on an overhead-line current of 1,500 d.c. and are

● LEFT
In 1996, a Mass Transit Railway (MTR) train speeds along one of the few open sections. This is on the Tsuen-Wan line serving this industrial centre in the New Territories (NT).

designed for maximum loading, their seating being lengthwise down the sides only. A four-car set can carry 3,000 people of whom only 400 can be seated.

● TUEN MUN LIGHT-RAIL TRANSIT (LRT)

The territory's population explosion transformed the rural NT. New towns have been built and modern public transport is essential. The history is complex but the result is the Tuen Mun Light-Rail Transit (LRT), a 31.75 km (19.7 mile) network operated by single-ended cars sometimes paired in multiple. The 1201 Series are called "drones", because they are powered but do not have full driving capability. The first phase – 23 km (14 miles) between Tuen Mun in Castle Peak Valley and Yuen Long – was opened on 18 August 1988. The system is run by the Kowloon-Canton Railway Corporation (KCRC).

● LEFT
Hong Kong Tramways tram No. 90 en route in 1991. Such sections of street running have much delayed trams in frequently congested traffic.

AUSTRALASIA

With the coming of the 1950s, the writing was on the wall for those fiery steeds that had served railways for more than a century: growling tin boxes on wheels were on the horizon. Steam locomotives were still built for Australian Railways for a few more years, however. Class BB13 1/4, No. 1089 was the last for Queensland in 1958. These final steamers, still needed by the community to overcome the problems created by the years of World War II, had very short lives.

● DIESEL-ELECTRICS

With the arrival of diesel-electrics, much individuality disappeared from the railway systems as they began to buy what were basically standard overseas designs, just like those in the automotive trade. These designs were modified to suit local gauge, track and climatic conditions, but between systems they varied by little more than colour schemes. A few steam-builders tried to enter the field. Beyer Peacock with Metropolitan Vickers of Manchester produced 48 2-Do-2 locomotives for Western Australia Railways (WAR) in 1954, this arrangement giving a lightweight distribution over the track. With a few

● **ABOVE**
Tasmania, with a sudden rise in load sizes, had to obtain more powerful locomotives. The Z Class at 1,850 hp doubled the power of existing main-liners. These four Co-Co units entered traffic in 1972 and were a development of the Western Australian Railways (WAR) R Class. They were built locally under licence to English Electric and were followed by even more powerful units. The example's yellow colour scheme was intended to give better visibility at level crossings.

● **ABOVE RIGHT**
J & A Brown's 2-8-0 locomotive No. 23 was built at the Great Central Railway's Gorton Works in 1918. It is pictured hauling coal out of Sockrington en route to Port Waratah.

● **BELOW**
An Australian heavy-hauled diesel-electric locomotive.

exceptions, the market soon rationalized itself to four main brands, mostly built under local licence – English Electric, Alco, General Motors-EMD (EMD) and General Motors of America (GM).

● FIRST MAIN-LINE DIESEL ELECTRICS

The first main-line diesel-electrics to go into service in Australia were 32 V Class Bo-Bos supplied by English Electric in Britain to the tiny island-state of Tasmania, which had joined the Australian Commonwealth in 1901. These were hood units with a cab at one end. With major water problems on the long desert run over the Nullabor Plain in South and Western Australia, Commonwealth Railways (CR) soon followed with 11 A1A-A1A GM units built under licence by the then-local firm of Clyde Engineering in 1951. These were single-ended, full-width units with a streamlined cab. At the same time, New South Wales (NSW) Railways imported

● RIGHT
New South Wales (NSW) Railways, to try to revive ever-decreasing country-passenger traffic, took the British high-speed train (HST) design and modified it for local conditions. The Paxman engines were retained but stainless-steel construction was used for the trains. The 19 Bo-Bo units of 2,000 hp were geared for 160 kph running. Here, a northbound XPT crosses Boanbee Creek Bridge on the north coast in 1990, about nine years after the first XPT train entered service.

40 A1A-A1A hood units, the 40 Class, from Alco in Canada. Overseas use of Bo-Bo units was common but Australia systems chose six-wheel bogies because of load limitations on the lighter track. From then on, the replacement of steam was rapid. NSW continued to favour Alco units, built locally, until the collapse of Alco in America in the late-1970s.

● **STATES SELECT BUILDERS**

Victoria soon became a GM state. Tasmania chose English Electric; South Australia, a mix of Alco and English Electric; Commonwealth Railways, GM; Western Australia GM and Queensland a mix of English Electric and GM. Because American designs eventually outnumbered the others and English Electric units were incompatible with the American, the building of EE locomotives in Australia ceased in 1976.

One local builder made an impact on the market, producing Bo-Bo diesel-hydraulic locomotives – Walkers Ltd of Maryborough, near Brisbane, Queensland: Emu Bay Railway bought four main-line units in 1963 and another seven in 1970; Queensland Railways (QR) bought 73 for shunting in 1968; the NSW Railways 50 in 1970 and WAR five in 1971. With the railways abandoning anything but block-loads, these shunters had a very short life as such. However, still being serviceable, most were sold off, and many were eventually converted to 2 ft gauge and put into service on the extensive Queensland sugar cane networks.

● RIGHT
Commonwealth Railways (CR) followed the WAR lead with its traffic increasing, in breaking the then 2,000-hp barrier. It ordered 17 3,000 hp CL Class locomotives in 1970. Following earlier policy, CR stayed with GM-EMD products. CR, unlike WAR, ordered a full-width streamlined body. Here, CL31 leads a mix of other classes on a heavy ore-train at Cockburn, south-west of Broken Hill, South Australia, in 1988. By then, CR had become Australia's National and swallowed the railways of South Australia and Tasmania.

A State Railways standard Class 2-8-2T engine, No. 26, pictured on the South Maitland Railway. Made by Beyer Peacock, these engines were nicknamed "Bobtails".

● BELOW
An advertisement by the Vulcan Foundry, showing one of the 60 J Class 2-8-0s supplied to Victorian Government Railways.

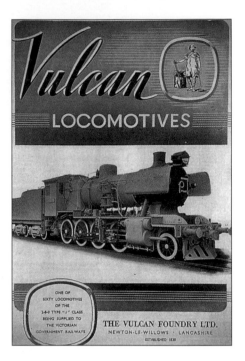

As to the trackwork in various states, not until 1987 did governmental lines consider anything more powerful than 2,000 hp. That year, WAR ventured into more power with 25 L Class Co-Co GM hood units, probably influenced by the private iron-ore lines in Western Australia, where superpower and record loads were seen as early as 1965. Since then, 4,000 hp has been reached on governmental lines with NSW obtaining 31 Co-Co units from GM-EMD in Canada, the 90 Class. The iron-ore lines are still ahead, with 29 GE Dash 438-hp locomotives having been imported from the Erie Railroad, USA.

Electrification did not advance far in most states. Queensland, however, with its tremendous mineral traffic, went into it in a big way. Since 1986 about 186 locomotives of the Bo-Bo-Bo wheel arrangement have entered traffic. This arrangement is unusual for Australia. These are all of 3,890 hp. Many have Locotrol transmitters, allowing trains to be run with several locomotives leading and several in the middle of loads. Loads often exceed 10,000 tonnes.

● NEW ZEALAND'S EXPERIENCE
New Zealand has passed through a similar period. It started with three

English Electric classes from 1952. These included one of the unusual wheel arrangement of 2-Co-Co-2, the Df Class, again a matter of distributing weight. However, GM gained the upper hand here also, in 1955, with the introduction

● LEFT
Coal is one of the main commodities handled by New South Wales (NSW) Railways. Two 4-8-4+4-8-4 (AD) 60 Class Garratts roar through Cockle Creek with a bulkload in 1970.

● RIGHT
This S Class GM20 A1A-A1A Co-Co unit is pictured in typical South Australian countryside, south-east of Lake Eyre on the Marree line.

of 146 Da Class A1A-A1A units. Most locomotives being imported, New Zealand shopped around. In 1968, Mitsubishi, Japan, supplied 64 Bo-Bo-Bo diesel-electrics to dieselize South Island.

With more power needed on North Island, 1972 saw the introduction of 49 Dx Class Co-Co units from GE. At 2,600 hp, three were large units for the 3 ft 6 in gauge. In 1993 work started on upgrading these units to 3,200 hp as the Dxr Class. New Zealand Railways has now been privatized, and sold to America's Wisconsin Central Railway (WCR), which has turned it into a progressive, profitable enterprise.

● PRIVATIZATION

The announcement of the intended sale of the National Rail (NR) freight system left an uncertain future for 120 NR Class, 4,000 hp Co-Cos recently ordered from GM and for their builders Goninan & Co, which delivered the first of these powerful locomotives.

STATE RAILWAY AUTHORITY, NEW SOUTH WALES (NSW) CLASS 48

Date	1959
Builders	Alco/Goodwin/GE/AEI
Client	NSW State Railway
Driving wheels	Co-Co
Total weight	75 tonnes
Rated power	708 kW
Maximum speed	120 kph

● LEFT
In South Australia a 48 Class Alco locomotive, No. 872, works a goods-train at Minnipa on the isolated narrow-gauge Port Lincoln Division, Eyre Peninsula.

AUSTRALIAN LIGHT RAIL AND METRO

Australia is one of the most urbanized countries in the world, with 70 per cent of its population living in towns and cities. The cites are concentrated in the coastal regions in the east and south. This is where the major cities – Sydney (New South Wales), Melbourne (Victoria), Brisbane (Queensland) and Adelaide (South Australia) – have developed. An exception is on the other side of the continent, Perth (Western Australia).

● TRAMWAYS NOT METROS

None of Australia's major cities has a dedicated metro system, although the electrified urban-rail networks in both Melbourne and Sydney fulfil a similar role to some extent, with city-centre underground loops linked to suburban lines.

● RIGHT
Adelaide Tram No. 376 dates from 1929. It is pictured on the street track through the shopping centre at Glenelg seaside suburb. The pantograph is part of recent modernization.

Tramways appeared in 13 Australian towns and cities in the late 19th and early 20th centuries. After World War II, uneconomic tramways in smaller towns were replaced by buses. In the 1950s and 1960s, all major cities apart from Melbourne followed the British trend to wholesale tramway abandonment. In Adelaide, one tram route has survived, the reserved track linking the city centre with Glenelg seaside suburb. This is operated by light modernized trams of 1929 vintage. Proposals for a new light-rail line in Adelaide were superseded by the project for the O-Bahn guided busway, opened in 1983. Debate continues about new rolling stock for the Glenelg line and its extension across the city centre to northern Adelaide.

● SOUTHERN HEMISPHERE'S LARGEST TRAMWAY

Melbourne's 238km (148 mile) tramway is the largest in the Southern Hemisphere. It has seen significant expansion in recent years as well as new rolling stock to replace most of the

MELBOURNE CLASS Z TRAM

Date	1974–7
Builders	Comeng/ASEA
Client	Melbourne Tram
Gauge	1,435 mm
Power supply	600 volt d.c.
Bogie arrangement	Bo-Bo with four 52 kW motors
Maximum speed	70 kph

● LEFT
Melbourne's Z Class trams were the first modern cars to enter service in quantity. Tram No. 110 is seen on the recent extension to Latrobe University.

● **RIGHT**
A prototype double-deck train for Victorian Railways, destined to operate on Melbourne's suburban system, runs into Heatherdale Station in the eastern suburbs.

● **BELOW**
Bourke Street in Melbourne shows articulated-trams on light-rail service operating through a pedestrianized area.

● **BOTTOM**
"Toast-rack" Tram No. 17 returns to the depot after private-hire duty on this heritage tramway running through the streets of Bendigo (formerly Sandhurst) in Victoria State. Bendigo was a Gold Rush town, founded in 1851.

traditional centre-entrance bogie trams. However, some of these are being refurbished for further use, including those on the City Circle line, which offers free travel around the central area. Changes from trolley-pole to pantograph current-collection and to one-man operation across the system are nearing completion. Most routes use modern bogie-trams and articulated-cars. The latest extensions and the recent conversion of rail lines to the St Kilda and Port Melbourne districts are built to light-rail standards.

In Sydney, a new tramline has been constructed to link the central railway station with the Darling Harbour redevelopment district. This was partly privately financed and is worked by Australia's first low-floor trams, the articulated Variotram design from ADtranz. Darling Harbour is also the site of a privately owned monorail offering a tourist link to the city centre's edge.

● **MUSEUM MOVEMENT**

The tramway-museum movement is well established in Australia. The operations in Adelaide (St Kilda), Ballarat in south-central Victoria and Sydney (Loftus) include alignments in or beside the public highway. In Bendigo, central Victoria, the tramway museum runs a daily heritage service carrying passengers between tourist attractions using street track through the town centre.

SOUTHERN AFRICA

Steam-locomotive deliveries to the Republic of South Africa (Union of South Africa, 1910–61) continued until the late 1960s.

● **SOUTH AFRICA'S KAROO DESERT**
The most dramatic post-World War II design was the 90 Class 25 condensing 4-8-4s of 1953. These were based on the 15F Class 4-8-2s, with large boilers, cast-steel integrated bed-frames and roller bearings throughout. Also built were 50 condensing engines classified 25NC.

The condensers, used for services on the main line through the arid Karoo desert of Cape Province, could save up to 85 per cent of their water consumption, a far cry from the early days when water had to be taken into the desert by train. The condensers had no conventional exhaust beat, only the whine of turbine-driven fans, which exhausted hot gases from the smokebox. The long banks of

condensing elements in the engine's tender made the locomotives 33 m (108 ft) long.

● **LAST GREAT GARRATTS**
The next year, 25 GO Class 4-8-2 + 4-8-4 Garratts were delivered from Henschel of Germany as a lighter variation on the GMA type. The Republic's last Garratts were for the 2 ft gauge lines delivered in 1967–68, built by Hunslet Taylor, of Alberton, SA. These were the last Garratt

● **ABOVE**
In Cape Province, an SAR Class 24 2-8-4 Berkshire heads along the scenic branch line between residential George and Knysna, skirting the Indian Ocean. This is one of South Africa's most scenic lines. The Class 24s, with light axleloading, are ideal for such routes. These engines were introduced in 1948 to replace the multitude of ever-ageing 6th, 7th and 8th classes.

● **BELOW LEFT**
An SAR 25 NC Class Condensing 4-8-4 locomotive heads a freight-train through the Karoo. These engines were introduced for services throughout the Cape Province's waterless desert, especially between Touws River-Beaufort West and Beaufort West-De Aar. Exhaust-steam from cylinders is not blown into the atmosphere but conveyed to the tender, where it is condensed in an air-cooling system and recycled into the boiler.

SAR CONDENSER 25 NC CLASS 4-8-4

Date	1953
Builder	Henschel, Germany; North British, Glasgow, Scotland
Client	South African Railways (SAR)
Gauge	3 ft 6 in
Driving wheels	5 ft
Capacity	Cylinders 24 x 28 in
Total weight in full working order	234 tons

● ABOVE
South Africa's Red Devil 4-8-4 represented an attempt to improve steam-locomotive potential in the face of the avowed policy to eliminate steam-traction.

● LEFT
Painted in Imperial Brown, to match the coaching stock, Locomotive No. A371 glints in the sun at Figtree, south-west of Bulawayo, Zimbabwe (formerly Rhodesia), in 1993.

locomotives built. In contrast with the foregoing designs, a batch of 100 heavy-duty 0-8-0 shunting-locomotives was delivered from Krupp in 1952–53.

● RAPID MODERNIZATION
Motive-power modernization occurred as rapidly in South Africa as it had in so many other countries. The Republic was the preferred location for steam operations throughout the 1970s and most of the 1980s, attracting huge numbers of enthusiasts to see big steam locomotives in glorious landscape with idyllic weather conditions.

It had been hoped that the 25 NC 4-8-4s would be retained in Cape Province on the main line between De Aar, an important railway junction of main lines from Cape Town, Port Elizabeth and Kimberley, the world's diamond centre. The engines were relatively new and performing excellently. This was not to be and the changeover from steam has coincided with a partial rundown of the railway itself. On a happier note, South Africa retains enough steam operations to entice the visitor. These include some of the world's last Pacific 4-6-2s, active in industrial service on the goldfields.

● BELOW
A Landau Colliery Class 12A 4-8-2 heads a loaded train from the colliery to the connection with the South African Railway (SAR) main line. Landau, in common with many Transvaal collieries, used locomotives of main-line proportions. The 12As hauled 900 ton-trains over the steeply graded route.

● SOUTH AFRICA AND NAMIBIA

South Africa has abundant cheap coal but no oil, so electrification was the preferred form of motive power. An early candidate was predictably the suburban service around Johannesburg, in Transvaal, Africa's largest city south of Cairo, and in the Witwatersrand, the world's richest goldfields, and Cape Town, South Africa's legislative capital and the first white settlement in southern Africa (1652). The lines of Namibia (formerly South West Africa) were the first to be dieselized, as early as the late 1950s, because of the waterless terrain. Prevalent among South Africa's diesel fleet are the D34.400 Class/35.200 Class of diesel-electric Co-Cos. Among electric locomotives are Class 6E1 Bo-Bos. Unlike the previous steam fleet, the nation's diesels and electrics are being built mainly in South Africa.

Vast tonnages are being conveyed compared with loads in steam days. The main freight line in Cape Province is the 865 km (537 mile) route from the Iron

● **ABOVE**
A former EAR Governor Class Garratt 4-8-2＋2-8-4, with an 11-ton axleloading, plies across the frail line between Voi, the Kenyan railway junction on the Mombasa-Nairobi line, and Moshi, the Tanganyikan town on the slopes of Mount Kilimanjaro. This engine, No. 6024, is the Sir James Hayes-Sadler. The Governors, named after British colonial governors, comprised a class of 29 locomotives, all built in 1954, of which 12 were made under licence from Beyer Peacock, by Franco-Belge in Paris.

● **BELOW**
A Zambian freight-train arriving at the Victoria Falls on the Zambezi River at the Zimbabwe-Zambia border.

● **ABOVE**
In Tanzania, an EAR Class 31 Tribal 2-8-2 heads away from Tabora, a modern town founded in 1820 by Arabs. These engines have an 11-ton axleloading for the lightly graded lines of East Africa and were built by the Vulcan Foundry, Lancashire, England, in the mid-1950s. The class is named after East African tribes. This engine is No. 3129, Kakwa.

and Steel Corporation's mine at Sishen in Griqualand West to Saldanha on the coast north of Cape Town. This section is electrified on a 50 kV, single-phase a.c. system, and 9E Class Co-Co locomotives with an output of 5,070 hp haul trains up to 2.4 km (1½ miles) long. A motorcycle is carried on the leading locomotive for use when inspection of the train is needed.

● PROGRESS IN ZIMBABWE

In neighbouring Zimbabwe, steam-traction continued until the late 1950s when the last of the huge 20th Class 4-8-2＋2-8-4 Garratts was delivered. Since then, steady progress towards diesel-electrics of both Bo-Bo and Co-Co types has been made. These mixed with the steam fleet through the 1980s. It was thought this situation would continue. By 1996, however, all but a handful of the steamers had been withdrawn. Almost all of Zimbabwe's steam fleet over its last 20 years of operation were of the Garratt type.

● DRAMATIC END IN EAST AFRICA

A similar situation occurred over the territories covered by the former East African Railway Corporation (EARC). Steam ended dramatically with the 34

MOUNTAIN CLASS GARRATT

Date	1955
Builder	Beyer Peacock, Manchester, England
Client	East African Railways (EAR)
Gauge	Metre
Driving wheels	4 ft 6 in
Capacity	4 cylinders 20½ x 28 in
Total weight in full working order	222 tons
Tractive effort	83,350 lb

● **LEFT**
A mighty Class 59 4-8-2+2-8-4 Garratt climbs the steep coastal escarpment above Mombasa on the Indian Ocean at the start of its 535 km (332 mile) journey to Nairobi, the Kenyan capital. During this steeply graded journey, the Mountain Class engines take 1,200 ton trains and climb almost one mile in altitude, Nairobi being on a plateau 1,500 m (5,000 ft) above sea level. The engine shown is No. 5933, Mount Suswa.

Mountain Class 4-8-2＋2-8-4 Garratts of 1955. These 252 oilfired giants with a 21-ton axleloading worked from the Mombasa-Nairobi line. They were 32 m (104 ft) long and had a boiler of 7 ft 6 in diameter, more than twice the width of the tack gauge, and an 83,350 lb tractive effort. Incredible though this is for metre-gauge operation, a 372-ton 4-8-4＋4-8-4 locomotive was proposed with a 25-ton axle loading but the attraction of diesel-electrics prevented these Garratts from being built. Delivery of Tribal 2-8-2/2-8-4 Types continued until the mid-1950s when all-out dieselization began across the then British-controlled territories of Kenya, Uganda and Tanganyika.

● **STEP TOWARDS PAN-AFRICAN NETWORK**

One of the most dramatic events in Africa was the Tanzania-Zambia Railway – known as TAZARA and TANZAM – built in the 1960s to a 1,067 mm gauge. With a 1,860 km (1,155 mile) route length the line runs from Dar es Salaam to Kapiri Mposhi in the Zambian Copperbelt, north of the Zambian capital Lusaka. China provided the finance,

technical support and Bo-Bo diesel-hydraulics. This route serves export and import traffic between the Indian Ocean and Botswana, Malawi, Zaire, Zambia and Zimbabwe. The vision's potential has not been reached because of endemic economic and political problems but the railway is a tangible step towards the Pan-African railway network the continent so desperately needs.

● **BELOW**
In 1953–4, Beyer Peacock, of Manchester, England, delivered very British-looking locomotives to the then Southern Rhodesia (at that time part of the central African Federation with Northern Rhodesia and Nyasaland). One of them, a Rhodesian Railways 14A Class 2-6-2＋2-6-2 Beyer Garratt, pauses in Matabeleland for refreshment at Balla Balla on its way from West Nicholson to Bulawayo.

NORTHERN AFRICA

Desert condition in Algeria made dieselization inevitable, and steam disappeared in favour of American diesels in the 1950s. Electrification had begun in 1932 on iron-ore lines with about 40 electric-locomotives active.

● NORTH AFRICA – ELECTRIFICATION AND DIESELIZATION

In Morocco (El Maghreb el Aqua, the "Far West"), electrification began as early as 1927. Today, 50 per cent of the nation's railways are electrified. The system is modern, having overhead 3 kV d.c. Non-electrified sections are all diesel-operated.

Tunisia operates an intensive suburban service from Tunis, the capital, on standard and metre gauges. The country has a long-term statutory commitment to reopen lines and build new lines of metre and standard gauge.

Egyptian railways have been dieselized during the past 20 years. Freight has declined but passenger traffic is healthy. Investment in double-tracking, reopening of abandoned lines and the building of new lines is all taking place. About 350

● **ABOVE**
Trams at Helwân, the town and baths on the Nile in Lower Egypt, opposite the ruins of Memphis.

● **RIGHT**
A Class 500 4-8-2 of Sudan Railways, one of 42 engines built in the 1950s by North British of Glasgow, Scotland. Although 3 ft 6 in gauge, they have a 35,940 lb tractive effort, almost identical with that of an LMS Stanier 8F 2-8-0. The engine is pictured heading across the line between Kosti, in the Blue Nile Province, south of Khartoum, and Khana.

● **BELOW**
The Location Locomotive Works of Ghana Railways displays a contrast of diesel-electrics.

diesel-locomotives are on the books of Egyptian State Railways (ESR).

The 42 oilfired Class 500 4-8-2s supplied to Sudan by North British works, Glasgow, Scotland, were that builder's last big steam order and also the last placed by Sudan Railways.

Dieselization of main-line trains began in 1959 with a class of English Electric Co-Cos, which bear a striking resemblance to British Rail's Peaks. No sections are electrified. Sudan Railways is mainly diesel-operated but does use steam for some line work, particularly in the south with Class 500s and lightly axleloaded Pacifics and Mikados.

● **RIGHT**
An Algerian National Railways (SNCFA) 3 kV
d.c. Co-Co electric-locomotive. These operate
over a 256 km (159 mile) route between
Tèbessa, near the Algerian-Tunisian border,
and 'Annaba on the Mediterranean Sea.

● **BOTTOM LEFT**
An industrial diesel working in Ghana, West
Africa. Before independence in 1957, the
territory was known as Gold Coast.

● **BOTTOM RIGHT**
A Co-Co English Electric diesel of Sudan
Railways waits to leave Khartoum with the
15.50 hrs freight-train to Sennar Junction
between the White Nile and the Blue Nile
in 1981.

ALGERIAN RAILWAYS CO-CO ELECTRIC

Date	1972
Builders	Mechanical: LEW Electrical: Skoda
Client	Algerian National Railways (Société Nationale des Chemins de Fers Algériens) (SNCFA)
Gauge	Standard
Line current	3 kV d.c.
Rated output	2,700 hp
Length	18,640 mm
Weight	130 tons

● **WEST AFRICA – OBLIVION AND
WILLPOWER**

Sierra Leone is the largest, most-popu-
lated country to have lost its railways
altogether. The system comprised 515 km
(320 route miles). As recently as 1955,
4-8-2＋2-8-4 Garratt locomotives were
supplied by Beyer Peacock of Manchester,
England. In later years, the system also
received diesel-hydraulics. After Sierra
Leone's independence from Britain in
1961, the railway fell rapidly into oblivion.

The same could have happened in
Ghana but a national will to retain the
railway against massive economic and
operational odds prevailed and the system
is fighting back from the brink of ruin. All
the once-elegant steam locomotives have
vanished, to feed Ghana's large steel plant
at the seaport town of Tema. Diesel
locomotives operate all services. Some
Ghana Railways engineers feel that the
simplicity of steam locomotives was better-
suited to Ghanaian conditions than more
complex diesel-electrics. This sentiment is
often expressed in developing countries.

West Africa's largest railway network
was in Nigeria. The plenitude of oil,
however, meant massive competition
from road transport. This greatly eroded
the railway's premier place. In the 1980s,
the system was down to only 50 operable
main-line diesels. As in Ghana, the railway
is making a comeback with foreign aid.

GLOSSARY

Articulation
The connection of two or more parts of the otherwise rigid frame using pivots, to increase flexibility and allow the locomotive to take sharper curves.

Axleloading
The weight imposed on the track by the locomotive's heaviest pair of wheels.

Bar-frame
A structure of girders, instead of steel plates, on which the wheels and boiler are mounted.

Big three
Baldwin, Alco and Lima, the three principal builders of locomotives in America.

Bogie
A truck with a short wheelbase at the front of the locomotive, pivoted from the main frame.

Brick arch
An arch of firebricks in the firebox, which deflects the hot gases and distributes them evenly among the flue tubes.

Caprotti valve-gear
A locomotive valve-gear for regulating the intake and emission of steam. It uses two pairs of valves operated by cams whose angle can be varied to adjust the cut-off.

Class
A category of locomotives built to a specific design.

Compound locomotive
A locomotive in which the expansion of the steam is carried out in two stages, first in a high-pressure and then in a low-pressure cylinder, arranged in series.

Condensing locomotive
A type of locomotive used in areas where water is not easily available, in which exhaust steam is condensed and recycled as feedwater for the boiler.

Conjugated valve-gear
An arrangement in three-cylinder locomotives by which the valve-gear of the inside cylinder is worked by a system of levers connected to those of the outside cylinders.

Coupled wheels
The driving wheels together with the wheels joined to them by the coupling-rod. This arrangement enables the power to be spread over several wheels, thereby reducing wheel-slip.

Cowcatcher
A semi-vertical plate or grid above the rails at the front of the locomotive designed to push obstructions off the tracks in order to prevent derailments. Called a "pilot" in America.

Cross-stretcher
A girder or plate joining the main plates of the frame to give rigidity.

Cut-off
The point in the piston stroke at which the admission of steam is stopped.

Cylinder
One of two, three or four chambers in the locomotive, each containing a piston, which is forced backwards and forwards by the admission of high-pressure steam alternately on each side of it through steam ports controlled by valves.

Diagram
The work schedule of the locomotive.

Double-header
A train pulled by two locomotives.

Firebox
The part of the boiler that contains the fire, with a grate at the bottom; the sides and top are surrounded by water spaces.

Fireless locomotive
A locomotive with a boiler charged with steam from a separate source.

Footplate
The floor of the cab on which the crew stands, or the running-plate.

Frame
The structure of plates or girders that supports the boiler and wheels.

Franco-Crosti boiler
A boiler with a pre-heater drum to heat the feedwater, by means of exhaust steam and hot gases piped from the smokebox.

Gauge
The size of the track, measured between the insides of the rails.

Grate area
The interior size of the firebox at grate level, used as a measure of steam-raising capability.

Heating surface
The total surface area of the firebox, flue tubes and superheater elements.

Outside-frame
A locomotive class in which the frame is outside the coupled wheels.

Outside valve-gear
A locomotive class in which the mechanism for opening and closing the steam admission valves lies outside the frame.

Piston valve
A valve for controlling steam admission and exhaust in the form of two short pistons, attached to a valve rod, which operate over steam ports with a cylindrical profile.

Plate frame
The main frame of the locomotive consists of two thick steel plates, slotted to accommodate the axleboxes of the driving and coupled wheels.

Route availability
The tracks available to any class of locomotive, determined by its weight and other dimensions.

Running-plate
The footway that runs around the sides and front of the boiler.

Saddle-tank
A saddle-tank or saddleback locomotive has a tank that straddles the boiler.

Side tank
A tank locomotive with its tanks on the main frame at each side of the locomotive.

Slide valve
A valve for controlling steam admission and exhaust shaped like a rectangular lid.

Smokebox
The front section of the boiler, through which hot gases from the fire escape through the chimney and exhaust steam is expelled through the blastpipe below. The door at the front allows cinders to be cleared out.

Superheater
Superheater elements subject the steam to an extra heating on its way to the cylinders, so that even though its temperature drops in the cylinders it will remain sufficiently hot not to condense.

Tank locomotive
A locomotive that carries its fuel and water in bunkers and tanks attached to the main frame, not in a separate tender.

Tracking
A term describing the locomotive's ability to negotiate curved or irregular track.

Tractive effort (TE)
The force that the wheel treads of a locomotive exert against the rails: a measure of pulling-power.

Type
A category of locomotives conforming in function and basic layout, including wheel arrangement.

Valve-gear
The linkage connecting the valves of the locomotive to the crankshaft.

Vertical cylinder
A locomotive in which the cylinders are mounted in a vertical position.

Walschaert's valve-gear
A valve gear co-operated by a link, which is rocked to and fro by a return crank connected to the piston rod and a combination lever connecting the crosshead and the radius rod.

Wheel arrangements
The various combinations of leading, coupled and trailing axles are described by a three-figure formula known as the Whyte notation. The first figure refers to the leading wheels, the second to the coupled wheels and the final figure to the supporting wheels.

INDEX

CONVERSION CHART

To convert:	Multiply by:
Inches to centimetres	2.540
Centimetres to inches	0.3937
Millimetres to inches	0.03937
Feet to metres	0.3048
Metres to feet	3.281
Miles to kilometres	1.609
Kilometres to miles	0.6214
Tons to tonnes	1.016
Tonnes to tons	0.9842